WELCOME TO
thelocalscookbook

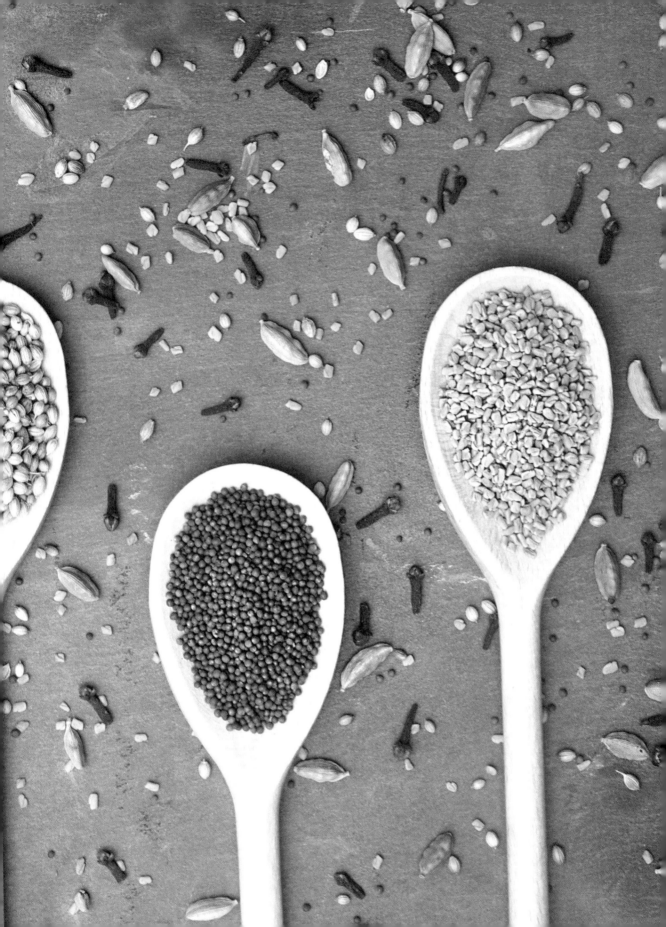

10% OF ALL PROFIT GOES BACK TO THE LOCALS

Editor: Jon Lewin
Food Styling: Jon Lewin
Words © Jon Lewin, 2015
Design © Jon Lewin, 2015
Copy Editor: Sophie Missing
All Photography © Jon Lewin, 2015
Except p8(bottom) © Dave Jones 2015
p8 (top), p265, p376, p377 © Ben Wyeth 2015
p5, p336(bottom right) © Johan Otterdahl 2015
Published by The Locals Cookbook Ltd
Printed by Graphicom, Italy

www.jonlewin.com
www.tasty-adventures.com

ISBN: 978-0-9934597-0-2

www.thelocalscookbook.com

CONTENTS

TheFood

TheRest

NOTES

Unless stated otherwise:
Spoon measures are heaped
1 tsp = 5ml spoon
1 tbsp = 15ml spoon

Herbs are fresh
Pepper is black and freshly ground
Salt is sea salt

All timings are provided as guidelines.

SOME ESSENTIAL INGREDIENTS

• vegetable oil • coconut oil • turmeric powder • cardamon pods • cumin seeds
• fenugreek seeds • oyster sauce • soya sauce • mustard seeds • white vinegar
• small dried fish • cinnamon sticks • rice flour • coconut milk • chilli powder
• curry powder • roasted curry powder • ground black pepper • chilli flakes
• maldive fish flakes • red split lentils • dill seeds • sea salt • goraka

Although you may have to splash out a bit initially, once you have the essentials, you'll be able to enjoy a Sri Lankan feast whenever you please. Turn to the Glossary (p394) for more information on where to find these ingredients.

SPICE RATINGS

0 – Not hot in the slightest
1 – Super mellow
2 – A little kick
3 – Tastebud teaser
4 – Packs a punch
5 – Hot hot hot

Gluten free

Dairy free

Vegetarian

HOW TO EAT

In Sri Lanka the only way to eat is with your hands – specifically your right hand. Aside from the cultural reasons for this, the food actually tastes better eaten this way! Without any lingering plastic or metallic taste from cutlery, you can enjoy Sri Lanka's finest dishes at their very best.

Sounds messy, right... It is at first, but you'll find that the more you practise the better you get and the difference in taste is well worth it. Of course, always wash your hands before eating.

I'd like to dedicate this book to my Mum
and to my best friend Charlie who got me
into cooking and surfing in the first place.
Rest in Peace.

The Author

MY JOURNEY

My culinary journey began at a very young age when I used to help my mum in the kitchen at home. She taught me a variety of techniques and recipes that ignited my love of cooking. Later, towards the end of my teens, I began training at Raymond Blanc's restaurant Le Manoir aux Quat'Saisons. I wasn't there for very long but it was a truly inspirational experience that fuelled my passion for food – and I've worked in many different kitchens across the world in the years since.

I've always had a keen interest in foreign cuisine and exotic ingredients. Travelling from a young age has given me a unique opportunity to see and taste the delights that far off destinations have to offer. Returning home after my travels, I would often find myself heading out to a restaurant to eat the same type of food I'd been enjoying overseas. I'd nearly always be disappointed by the fact that most of the dishes had been adapted to suit Western palettes, losing their authenticity in the process. This was when the concept of The Locals' Cookbook came to me: a series of books that would bring the true tastes of these idyllic corners of the world to a wider audience.

I believe that the two best ways to get an insight into a country and its culture are by eating the local food and interacting with the people. The Locals' Cookbook: Sri Lanka combines authentic recipes with informative first-hand accounts of my life immersed in this truly fascinating culture.

It is the first in a series of travel documentary style cookbooks that follow my journeys across the world, documenting the culture, food, stories, and recipes of the people I meet on my way. During my time in Sri Lanka, I lived with local families, experiencing the country at a grassroots level, from playing cards with the local fishermen, to trekking through the highlands to find the perfect tea. The authentic recipes I discovered on the way really are phenomenal and I hope you enjoy them as much as I do.

It's been a fantastic journey and one I plan to repeat with each country in the series.

SUN, SEA, SURF & MY LOVE OF PHOTOGRAPHY

I love being by the sea, whether I'm in it, foraging in rock pools or just cooking on the beach. I first went surfing with my Uncle Pat when I was 16 years old, and I haven't stopped since. It is the only thing that has kept me level throughout my life, regardless of the problems I've been faced with and it's taken me to many exotic destinations across the world.

I enjoyed the more creative side of things at school and made the best of it by studying art, design technology and business studies, which set me on my journey to becoming a photographer.

I then went on to do a degree in photojournalism at Swansea University to develop my photographic style (of course I chose a place by the sea so I could surf too!). I'd get my student loan, buy a plane ticket, and I'd be off for months at a time to Morocco, Central America, Sri Lanka or wherever else I fancied.

Cooking up a fresh seafood feast down Oxwich Bay.

Surfing at home on the Gower.

LIVING THE SIMPLE LIFE

Having spent over 2 years out of the last decade in Sri Lanka and having adapted to the way of life there, I wanted to try and live in a similar way back in the UK. Six years ago I bought a 26-year-old static caravan for the small sum of £300. I renovated it, starting from scratch. I now live between my little caravan on the Gower Peninsula in South Wales and Bristol where I am working with local businesses.

When I'm on the Gower I live completely off the grid with no running water or mains electricity. This makes life a little more difficult in terms of having to collect water and chop wood for the fire every day, but I find it hugely satisfying and am focused on my journey to self-sufficiency.

On the farm in Wales, where my caravan is, I have a thriving vegetable garden and a small collection of livestock. Living the outdoor life, I also hunt and forage, and have acquired the skills to process livestock from field to fork.

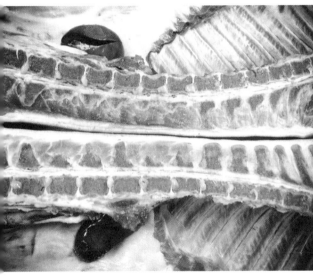

My little house on the
Gower Peninsular in
South Wales.

Mother Nature

THE POWER OF MOTHER NATURE

For most people, the Boxing Day Tsunami has become so interwoven with other distant global events that it has become just another disaster. For me, it was one of the most memorable events of my life. How the waves struck – and the impact they had – remains vividly engraved on my mind.

I first visited the beautiful teardrop island in the Indian Ocean in 2004 while on a surf trip with friends, arriving just a few weeks before Christmas. My mate Benji had been to Sri Lanka before and he knew an amazing little place for us stay. Situated right in front of one of the best surf spots on the island, the beauty and hospitality of the Surfing Beach Guest House has drawn me back every year since. Noel and Ranji Panditha run the place and I consider them my second family. They have one son, Hasanka, who is like a little brother to me. In fact, I call him 'Mali' which means 'little brother' in Sinhalese (the main language spoken on the island).

We spent the first part of our trip exploring the different surf spots along the palm-fringed coastline and scored some epic waves, better than any I had experienced before. Christmas Day was no different: three epic sessions and one of the best Sri Lankan feasts I'd ever eaten.

We were pretty excited for Boxing Day, as some of the local surfers had told us that a big swell was coming that coincided with the full moon. Nothing could have prepared us for the magnitude of what was about to unfold. It was around 8am when I woke to the sound of people cheering from the balcony outside. I got up and noticed a little wave had come in and knocked everyone's breakfast off the tables. This was followed by a knock from Ranji at my bedroom door. When I walked out of my room there was mountains of white water coming towards me. I darted back and slammed the door shut; it was my first instinct. This wasn't the best thing to do; the pressure of the water swung the door back and I got caught behind it. My mate Thorney was still in bed, floating around the room – we didn't know what the hell was going on.

There hadn't been a Tsunami for a very long time, so it wasn't just us; no one knew what was happening. The water level in the room rose to about chest height before disappearing as quickly as it had arrived.

Hikkaduwa beach after the
first wave struck.

THE AFTERMATH

Everything was frantic: there were people shouting everywhere and we were doing our best to help dig out a girl trapped under rubble next door. I looked back and it was like someone had pulled a plug on the ocean – you could see the whole reef, which was really unusual as the tidal range in Sri Lanka is only about one metre. Some of the locals were on the reef collecting their possessions and even fish that had been stranded.

The shouting started again. There was a Costa Rican guy who'd been in a tsunami before; he knew the water would return at a rapid rate so he started warning everyone to head to higher ground. We ran to the highest building in sight and got to the top floor just in the nick of time.

The second wave was as bad as the first and after the initial impact we decided the building was unsafe, so we got down and took our chances wading through the fast flowing water, bricks and debris.

The locals were heading towards a nearby jungle track so we followed them over the railway line to higher ground, deep into the jungle, where we stayed until later in the day when we could assess the damage.

The third wave had been even worse than the previous two and the coastline was devastated. No one was up for staying near the beach that night and various families in the jungle put us up. All through the night, there were Chinese whispers about another wave and none of us really slept.

They gave up their own beds and shared what little food they had to eat. The kindness and warmth shown by the Sri Lankan people following the disaster was astonishing. They had so little to begin with, and following the Tsunami they had nothing. The genuine compassion and care that they showed taught me a lot.

From that moment, I felt a strong bond with the country and its people. I have returned to Sri Lanka every year since, and have built up some amazing friendships and family networks. It is a truly amazing culture, full of smiles, compassion and a general togetherness that I cannot find the words to adequately express.

Galle Road, Hikkaduwa.

This shot was taken on Boxing Day 2005, exactly a year after the tsunami. This memorial paddle out was held in rememberance on Hikkaduwa's main reef at the same time the waves struck.

Staples

ONE CURRY IS NEVER ENOUGH

If the common base of Italian and French cooking is onion, celery, and carrots (known as a soffritto or mirepoix) then in Sri Lankan cooking the base is usually green chilli, red onion, garlic and curry leaves.

Sri Lankans like to eat lots of differently flavoured small dishes. In a Sri Lankan house you never eat just one curry. It's common to prepare five or six different dishes every night – maybe one fish, one meat, and four veggie-based curries and then a dhal too. Just as we would eat naan bread with our curries here in the UK, in Sri Lanka you have flat breads, rotis or string hoppers.

Due to the country's diverse climate, in addition to the influence of South Indian, Portuguese, Dutch, Arab and British colonists, Sri Lankan food has endless combinations of flavour. Usually the mother or grandmother of a household will spend a large part of the day in the kitchen. Whoever is at the stove, it is this dedication to cooking – something we struggle with in our modern, convenience focused culture – which makes Sri Lankan food so distinctly different to what most of us are used to. Eating is not simply a way of filling your stomach, but a ritual that should be savoured and thoroughly enjoyed.

On my first trip to Sri Lanka, I became captivated by the super spicy, vibrant and delicious dishes on offer. At first, I found the sheer amount of spice used to be a real assault on the senses but my taste buds soon adapted and I'm now addicted!

If you're not so into the spice, be sure to go easy on the chilli powder, leave out a few chillies, or at the very least deseed them first.

ROASTED CURRY POWDER
Makes 175g's

50g coriander seeds
40g cumin seeds
25g fennel seeds
1½ tsp fenugreek seeds
½ tsp cardamom seeds
½ tsp black mustard seeds
1 tsp black peppercorns
½ tsp cloves
3 inch cinnamon stick
4 dried red chillies
a handful of dried curry leaves
2 inch piece of lemongrass
1 tbsp uncooked long grain rice

Place a large frying pan on a medium to high heat. Once hot, add coriander seeds and cook until they start to become golden brown in colour and smell fragrant.

Add the rest of your ingredients and continue to cook until they also turn golden brown. Keep a close eye on the pan as the whole spices can start to burn fairly easily – you just want to toast them lightly.

Put all ingredients into a pestle and mortar or a blender, and grind to a fine powder.

Use straight away or, as with the raw curry powder, store in a clean airtight container for up to 6 months. It does lose its pungency over time so I'd recommend you make it as and when you need it.

SERVES: 4 PREP TIME: 0 COOKING TIME: 20 SPICE: 3/5

USEFUL FACT: This definitely has to be my favourite blend of curry powder. It is extremely diverse and can be used in meat, seafood and vegetable dishes. It has a fantastic aroma that screams Sri Lankan cuisine.

COOKING RICE

There are many different varieties of rice but, as the most readily available are long grain and basmati, I am giving my cooking method for these. There are also many different ways to cook rice, but I find that this one is super simple and works a treat every time.

First, rinse your rice under running water until the water runs clear. Drain well – this will stop the rice from becoming too sticky and starchy.

Place a large pan of salted water on a medium heat and bring to the boil. Add the rice (I tend to use roughly 60-80g uncooked rice per person but adjust the amount according to personal preference).

Once the rice starts to dance around in the pan, boil for a further 5 minutes and then drain in a colander. Add 3½ cm of water back into the pan, bring back to the boil then turn down to a low heat and simmer gently.

Cover the top of your colander of rice with foil (or you could use a lid, if you have one that fits snugly) and place on top of your pan. This will steam the rice for the remainder of the cooking time and keep it nice and fluffy. Steam the rice for around 10 minutes, take off the heat and fluff up using a fork before serving.

USEFUL TIP: Try adding fresh herbs, lemon zest, a stick of cinnamon, or even a few cardamom pods when boiling the rice. They will infuse during the cooking process and give your rice a deliciously subtle flavour.

STRING HOPPERS

500g roasted rice flour
1 tsp salt
500ml hot water

Sieve the rice flour into a mixing bowl and add the salt.

Gradually add the water bit by bit and mix thoroughly by hand until a dough-like consistency is achieved. You may need a little extra water.

When it has come together, place a handful of the dough into the special string hopper press and push out in a circular motion on to the bamboo or plastic grates. Three times round should be enough.

After you have made around ten, fill the bottom part of a steamer with water then place on a high heat and bring to the boil.

Layer the grates around the top part of the steamer, moving in circles to ensure they are all cooked evenly.

Place the top part of the steamer on the bottom and cover with a lid.

Steam for around 8-10 minutes or until bouncy to the touch. Then take out and remove the string hoppers from the grates. Repeat until you have used up all your dough.

They can be served hot or cold – either way is fantastic.

SERVES: 4 PREP TIME:25 COOKING TIME: 20 SPICE: 0/5

HOPPERS & EGG HOPPERS

7g sachet of active yeast
3 tbsp sugar
100ml warm water
375g rice flour
1 tsp salt
2 x 400ml tins of coconut milk
2 tbsp coconut oil (optional)

Place yeast, sugar and water in a small bowl and mix together well. Leave for around 10 minutes to allow the yeast to do its thing.

Add the rice flour and salt to a large mixing bowl. Create a well in the centre and add the yeast mix together with the coconut milk. Whisk until you have a super smooth consistency, similar to pancake mix. Then set aside and allow to rest for half an hour.

Once rested, place a non-stick pan for which you have a lid on a low heat. If you don't have a non-stick pan, add coconut oil ensuring it coats the pan's surface evenly. Once hot, add half a ladle of your mixture. Spread around by picking up the pan and tilting it in all directions until the mixture has completely covered the surface.

Add the lid and cook for 2-3 minutes. Remove using a palette knife or flexible spatula. Serve hot or cold – either way is great.

To make egg hoppers: after 1 minute of the hopper cooking time, break an egg into the centre of the pan, season with salt and pepper then cover and cook until the egg is nice and firm.

Egg hoppers are great for breakfast served with coconut chilli sambol or any other time of the day with a variety of different curries.

SERVES: 4 PREP TIME: 10 COOKING TIME: 5 SPICE: 0/5

RAW CURRY POWDER

2 tsp fenugreek seeds
6 tbsp coriander seeds
2 tbsp cumin seeds
1 tsp fennel seeds
1 tsp black mustard seeds
5 sprigs curry leaves, dried
1 tsp whole black peppercorns
1 cinnamon stick
4 cloves

First place a large frying pan on a medium to high heat. Once hot, add the fenugreek seeds and cook until they start to pop and become golden brown in colour.

Add the toasted fenugreek seeds and all the other ingredients to a large pestle and mortar or a coffee grinder and grind to a fine powder.

Use straight away or it can be stored in a clean airtight container for up to 6 months.

PREP TIME: 10 COOKING TIME: 2 SPICE: 3/5

RICE FLOUR

1kg white or brown rice

Soak rice in water for 2-3 hours.

Drain off any excess water and place the rice on some kitchen towel, in a single layer, for around 45 minutes or until it has dried completely.

Once dry, crush the rice in a blender or using a pestle and mortar. With either method, it is best not to attempt to do all the rice at once, but to take a few handfuls at a time.

Add the crushed rice mixture to a fine meshed sieve and sieve into a large bowl. Any pieces that won't go through will need to be blended again.

Repeat this process until you have used up all the rice. Your rice flour is now ready to be used.

USEFUL TIP: Rice flour can easily be bought, but making it from scratch is super easy. Your homemade rice flour can be stored in a clean airtight container for months.

PARATHA FLATBREADS

250g plain flour
250g wholewheat flour
1 tsp salt
150ml vegetable oil
125ml water

Combine both types of flour and salt in a large bowl. Mix together using your fingers or a whisk. Create a small well in the middle of the flour and add a good glug of oil.

Next, add the water, a little at a time, and knead into a soft elastic dough. You may need a few extra tablespoons of oil if the dough feels tough. It should be soft and slightly sticky.

Knead the dough for around 60 seconds. Try not to knead for much longer than this as it will become too tough.

Place back into the mixing bowl, cover with oil and a wet tea towel and allow to rest at room temperature for approximately 1 hour.

Oil your work surface and divide the dough into eight equal balls then cover each with oil. Press the balls between your palms to flatten them, one at a time, creating a disc shape.

Continue flattening each disc on your oiled work surface, then pick up a disc and throw down on to the surface. (This action stretches the dough.) Repeat until the dough is paper-thin and then, starting at one end, fold the dough onto itself in 2cm strips, continuing until you get to the end.

Make a spiral with your dough and wrap around, tucking in the end underneath into the centre. Flatten into a circular disc using the palm of your hand one last time. Repeat for the remainder of your dough balls.

Place a large frying pan on a medium heat and add a few tablespoons of oil. Fry each paratha for a few minutes on each side and allow to cool slightly before serving.

SERVES: 4   PREP TIME: 25   COOKING TIME: 10   SPICE: 0/5

EXTRACTION OF COCONUT MILK

Many people think that coconut milk is the liquid inside a coconut. This is a common misconception: the milk is actually squeezed out from the white flesh, which has to be ground out using a coconut grinder.

In Sri Lankan cuisine the coconut is of great significance and you traditionally use different types of extracts when cooking – normally up to four in total. The first extract is thicker and creamier than the rest, and is usually added to dishes at the very end of the cooking, to finish them. The second, third and fourth extracts are used throughout the cooking process. Although these are still tasty, the first extract is the most potent and delicious. In some ways, the whole process is similar to the different pressing stages of olive, virgin olive and extra virgin olive oil.

To extract fresh coconut milk, first peel away the brown husk from the shell. Make sure you remove all of it so none ends up in the flesh.

Next, take a sharp knife and pierce one or more of the three black eyes found on the shell's exterior. Drain the coconut water and set aside. (This water is extremely nutritious and is packed with electrolytes and minerals so I always put it in the fridge and drink it once it is cool.)

Using the back of a relatively heavy knife or cleaver, place the coconut in your hand and carefully split in half. This can be quite difficult: if you don't feel comfortable doing it, then ask someone who does. Once you have the two halves you need to take out all the white flesh inside using a coconut grinder.

There are many ways to extract the milk, but for me, squeezing it by hand feels the most natural. Once you have removed all the flesh to a bowl, add half a cup of water. Grab a handful of the flesh and squeeze over a sieve and separate bowl, repeating the process until you've extracted all that you can. This is the first extract. You can repeat this process as many times as you like, but after the fourth I find the milk to be too weak, although it is still better than using water.

COCONUT FLATBREADS

300g plain flour
1 tsp salt
125ml water
150g freshly ground coconut flesh
1 red chilli, finely chopped
2 green chillies, finely chopped
1 red onion, finely chopped
1 tsp black pepper
2 tbsp coconut oil

Sift flour into a bowl then add salt, pepper and freshly ground coconut flesh. Mix together thoroughly by hand. Then slowly add in water and again mix by hand for around 5 minutes until fully combined.

Add the chopped chillies and red onion and continue to mix together until evenly distributed. Knead for a few minutes and then set aside. Cover with cling film and allow to rest at room temperature for 30 minutes.

Place a large frying pan on a medium heat and add 2 tablespoons of coconut oil. While the pan is heating up, split your dough into four equally sized balls and flatten by hand to around 1cm in thickness.

Fry one at a time for around 2-3 minutes on either side or until golden brown in colour. These are fantastic for breakfast or as an accompaniment to any number of curries.

SERVES: 6 PREP TIME: 35 COOKING TIME: 5 SPICE: 2/5

DEEP FRIED POPPADOMS

300g urad/urid flour
¼ tsp ground black pepper
¼ tsp ground cumin (optional)
¼ tsp salt
200ml water
500ml vegetable oil

Place the flour in a large mixing bowl then add black pepper, ground cumin and salt. Mix together with a wooden spoon then add the water, a little at a time – you may not need all of it – and knead until the dough comes together.

Flour your work surface. Take a golf ball-sized piece of dough and roll out using a rolling pin until it is a few millimetres thick. Take a 15cm pastry ring, place on to the rolled out dough and use to cut out circles (these are your uncooked poppadoms). Repeat until you have used up all the dough.

Take a wok or high-sided frying pan and place on a medium to high heat. Add the vegetable oil. Once it is sizzling hot, you are ready to start deep-frying. You can test the temperature by taking a small piece of dough and placing it into the oil. If it starts to bubble up immediately then you're good to go. Make sure to take care while deep-frying.

Fry a few poppadoms at a time. Give them a few minutes on the first side, to allow them to bubble up nicely and create the little air pockets inside. Then turn over using a metal spatula and fry for a further 30 seconds. Remove from the oil and drain on kitchen roll.

They can be eaten warm straight away or you can eat them later once they have cooled down – either way is great. Enjoy!

SERVES: 4 PREP TIME: 15 COOKING TIME: 3 SPICE: 0/5

USEFUL TIP: Add a teaspoon of cumin seeds to your dough to give it more flavour.

5am at a local bakery on the South East coast in Tissamaharama.

The Locals

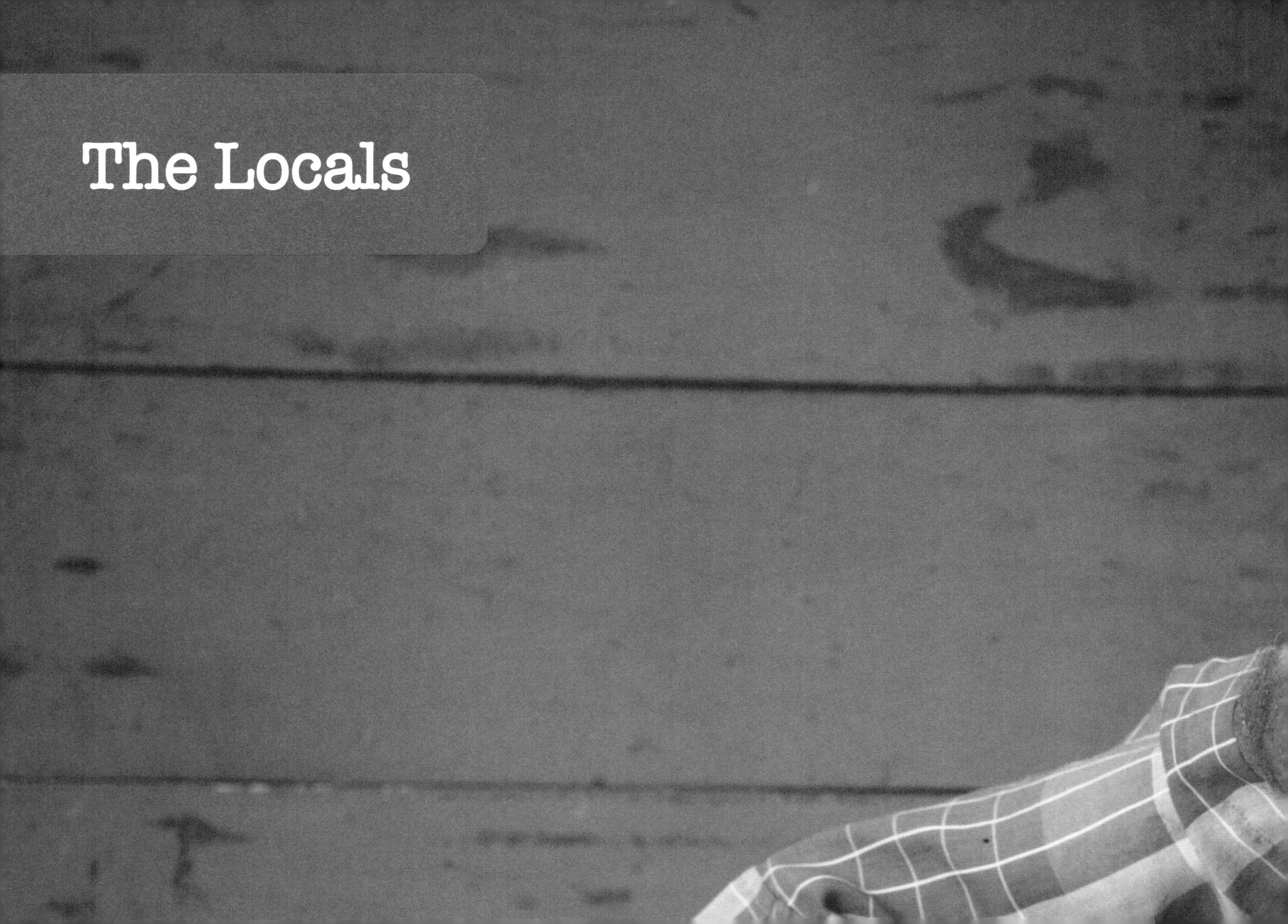

SRI LANKA IS THE EYES, SMILES & ACTIONS OF ITS PEOPLE

Sri Lanka is a country of the heart. This can be seen in the eyes, smiles and actions of its people. I have been around the world, and the Sri Lankan people are among the most welcoming, happy, and compassionate people I have met.

Having visited the island for over ten years now, I see many of the people I have met not only as my good friends but as my family too. Once you've visited you will see what I mean.

As with most places, speaking the local dialect goes a long way and gives you an instant connection with the people. Even if you just learn a few basic phrases, it's well worth it and you're sure to receive an even warmer welcome, if that's even possible.

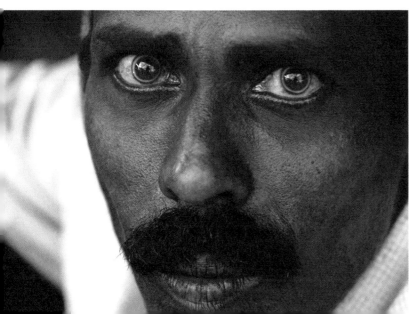

A COUNTRY OF THE HEART

Sri Lanka is a diverse country – ethnically, linguistically, and in terms of religion. Buddhism is the predominant religion but alongside the many Buddhist temples are Mosques, Hindu temples and Christian churches too. There is a lesson to be learnt from their tolerance and acceptance of other religions.

Warmth and kindness radiates from the people of Sri Lanka, whether it's the carefree smiling children, or the happy-go-lucky older generation. The Sri Lankans' warm and friendly nature is reflected in their constantly smiling faces. They are eager to help anyone unfamiliar with local life, hospitable to the extreme and take pride in inviting people to their homes, however modest they may be. So don't be surprised if a tuk-tuk driver or surf guide, or indeed anyone you encounter, requests the pleasure of your company. And try not to decline these offers, as Sri Lankan hospitality is taken very seriously!

Street Food

GREAT SNACKS FROM SMALL SHACKS

Although not as varied as neighbouring India, Sri Lankan street food encompasses a wide variety of snacks or 'short eats' as they are more commonly known. These include: rotis, hoppers, egg hoppers, curried fish rolls, kottu, delicious BBQ chicken and a whole lot more.

Street food is available all over the island, from the small shacks on the roadside, to the specially adapted carts that trundle through the streets day and night. Some dishes have a South Indian influence, but generally the tantalising combination of spices and flavours used makes Sri Lankan street food extremely unique.

The majority of street food is extremely spicy. So, if you are not comfortable with the slow burn of the chilli and spice, ask for one of the milder options available. Street food in Sri Lanka is extremely cheap, so if you find yourself a little strapped for cash, this is the way to eat.

SPICED CHICKPEAS WITH FRESH COCONUT

3 tbsp coconut oil
½ tsp black mustard seeds
3 dried red chillies,
roughly chopped
3 tbsp broken coconut pieces
2 sprigs fresh curry leaves
300g chickpeas
1 tsp salt

This is super easy and tastes amazing. If you are using dried chickpeas then you will need to soak them in cold water overnight and boil them in water for 30 minutes before frying. Canned chickpeas are fine to use too.

Place a wok or high-sided frying pan on a medium to high heat and add the coconut oil. Once it starts to sizzle, add the mustard seeds. When they start to spit in the pan, add the red chillies, curry leaves and coconut pieces.

Fry for 3 minutes then add the chickpeas and cook for a further 4 minutes, tossing occasionally.

Season with salt to taste and serve.

SERVES: 4 PREP TIME: 10 COOKING TIME: 10 SPICE: 2/5

ULUNDU VADAI

300g urid/urad dhal
6 cloves garlic, finely chopped
10 shallots, finely chopped
3 red onions, finely chopped
3 green chillies, finely chopped
3 sprigs fresh curry leaves,
roughly chopped
1½ tsp salt
1 tsp black pepper
500ml vegetable oil

Soak your dhal in water for around 3-4 hours. Drain thoroughly, place in a food processor and blend until you have a smooth paste. Set aside.

Next add the garlic, shallots, onions, green chillies and curry leaves to the dhal paste together with the salt and pepper and mix thoroughly by hand until everything is evenly distributed.

Lay a piece of cling film on a chopping board or work surface and take a golf ball sized amount of the mixture. Place on the cling film, flatten slightly with the palm of your hand then, using your finger, make a hole in the centre. Repeat this process until all of your mixture is used up.

Now place a wok on a low heat and add the vegetable oil.

Once the oil is hot – but not smoking, carefully peel your doughnuts from the cling film and place into the oil, a few at a time. Deep fry until golden brown, then drain on kitchen towel and allow to cool slightly before serving.

SERVES: 4 PREP TIME: 20 COOKING TIME: 15 SPICE: 1/5

USEFUL TIP: These savoury donuts are best sliced in half and served with green chilli coconut chutney (see p106).

DEEP FRIED DHAL FRITTERS

300g masoor dhal
500ml (plus 2 tbsp) vegetable oil
2 red onions, finely chopped
2 cloves of garlic, grated
2½ cm piece of ginger, grated
4 fresh green chillies, chopped
3 dried red chillies, chopped
30g Maldive fish flakes, crushed
3 sprigs fresh curry leaves
2½ tsp salt
1 tsp black pepper
2 tbsp water or coconut milk
(optional)
4 tbsp chickpea flour (optional)

Soak the dhal in water for a few hours or overnight. Personally, I tend to soak for 3-4 hours, as I like my lentils on the al dente side rather than mushy.

Once soaked, drain any excess water. Take three quarters of the soaked dhal and, using either a pestle and mortar or a blender, grind it into a paste. Mix in the remaining whole lentils, which will add a crunchy texture and variety.

Take a large frying pan and add the coconut oil. When sizzling, add the onions, garlic, ginger, chillies, fish flakes, curry leaves and seasoning. Fry for 3 minutes and then set aside to cool.

Add to the blended dhal and mix together thoroughly by hand. If the mixture is too dry add a few tablespoons of water or coconut milk; if it is too wet then you can add a bit of chickpea flour to help it combine.

Form the mixture into golf ball-sized pieces and flatten in the palm of your hand. Place a wok on a medium to high heat and add the coconut oil. When hot, start frying a few fritters at a time.

Once dark golden brown in colour, remove from the oil and drain on kitchen towel before serving.

SERVES: 4 PREP TIME: 25 COOKING TIME: 15 SPICE: 2/5

USEFUL FACT: If you want to mix things up a bit, try pressing a whole prawn into each ball before deep-frying.

SRI LANKAN SAMOSAS

2 tbsp coconut oil
1 tsp black mustard seeds
1½ tsp cumin seeds
6 cloves of garlic, grated
2½ cm piece of ginger, grated
3 sprigs fresh curry leaves
3 fresh green chillies, chopped
20 shallots, finely chopped
3 red onions, finely chopped
½ tsp chilli powder
1 heaped tsp curry powder
handful fresh coriander, chopped
1 tsp black pepper
1½ tsp salt
juice of a lime
500ml vegetable oil
1 egg

FOR THE PASTRY

400g plain flour
(plus extra for dusting)
1½ tsp salt
juice of ½ a lime
250ml warm water
50ml olive oil

Preparing the dough for the pastry is the messy bit. Take a large mixing bowl and sift in the flour then add the salt and water. Mix thoroughly by hand, squeezing the flour in your hands until it becomes crumb-like. Squeeze in the lime juice and then add the olive oil, a little at a time, mixing constantly. Your mixture should now have a dough-like consistency. Ensure that there is no flour stuck to the bottom of the bowl, then dust your work surface with flour and knead for around 10 minutes until it is smooth and elastic. Wrap in cling film and place in the fridge for 2 hours.

Place a large frying pan on a medium heat and add the coconut oil. Once sizzling, add the mustard seeds and, once they start to spit, add the cumin, garlic, ginger and curry leaves. Fry for 1 minute and then add the green chillies, shallots, onions, chilli powder, curry powder and coriander. Stir thoroughly to mix, and continue to fry until the onions soften and turn golden brown. Take off the heat, allow to cool and then add coriander. Mix thoroughly and set aside.

Take a chopping board – or use your kitchen surface – and dust generously with flour. Remove the dough from the fridge and divide into five equal portions. Using a rolling pin, roll each out until around ¼cm thick. Cut into long strips (around 10cmx15cm) and once each one is rolled, layer on top of each other and cover with a damp cloth to stop it drying out. cut as many as you can from the dough. Take any excess pastry, re-roll and repeat until you have used it all up.

Take a strip of dough and starting from the bottom right hand corner fold over to make a triangular shape leaving it to hang over the edge by 1cm. Then fold it onto itself maintaining a triangular shape and you will now have a nice little cone. Add 1½ tablespoons of the mixture to the cone and fold the remaining pastry. Once you get to the end, brush the edges with whisked egg and seal. Repeat this process until you have used up all the pastry.

Place a wok on a low to medium heat, add the vegetable oil and, once hot, add the samosas, a few at a time. It is important not to let the oil get too hot otherwise the outside of the samosa will cook too quickly. Fry until they are golden brown. Remove using a slotted spoon and drain on kitchen towel. These are best enjoyed fresh and warm.

SERVES: 4 PREP TIME: 25 COOKING TIME: 20 SPICE: 2/5

CHILLIED PINEAPPLE

300g fresh pineapple
(roughly ½ a pineapple)
1 level tsp chilli powder
1 tsp black pepper
1 tsp salt
1 tsp sugar
a squeeze of lime

This spicy but deliciously sweet street food snack is usually found on buses, trains and in little shacks.

Cut the pineapple into 2½ cm cubes and place on wooden skewers.

Add the remaining ingredients to a pestle and mortar and grind until mixed thoroughly. Cover the pineapple chunks in the mixture then squeeze over lime and enjoy.

SERVES: 2 PREP TIME: 10 COOKING TIME: 0 SPICE: 5/5

USEFUL TIP: Try using mango instead of pineapple or a combination of the two fruits.

BREADED SAMOSAS

150g potatoes, peeled & diced
2 tbsp coconut oil
1½ tsp cumin seeds
25 shallots, finely chopped
1 red onion, finely chopped
6 green chillies, finely chopped
8 cloves of garlic, grated
3 sprigs fresh curry leaves
1½ tsp salt
½ tsp black pepper
½ level tsp chilli powder
2 tsp roasted curry powder
500ml vegetable oil
4 eggs, whisked
half a loaf of bread,
(made into fine breadcrumbs)
juice of ½ a lime

FOR THE DOUGH

450g plain flour
(plus extra for dusting)
1½ tsp salt
4 tbsp ghee
juice of ½ a lime
250ml warm water

Take a large mixing bowl and sift in the flour then add the salt and water. Mix thoroughly by hand, squeezing the flour in your hands until it becomes crumb-like. Squeeze in the lime juice and then add the olive oil, a little at a time, mixing constantly. Your mixture should now have a dough-like consistency. Ensure that there is no flour stuck to the bottom of the bowl, then dust your work surface with flour and knead for around 10 minutes until it is smooth and elastic. Wrap in cling film and place in the fridge for 2 hours.

Boil the potatoes in salted water for 10-15 minutes, or until soft. Drain and mash then set aside.

Add the coconut oil to a pan over a medium heat. Once sizzling, add the cumin seeds, shallots, onion, chillies, garlic, curry leaves, salt and pepper, chilli powder and curry powder and fry until golden brown (keep an eye on them as they can burn easily). Add this mixture to the crushed potato and combine thoroughly by hand.

Take a chopping board – or use your kitchen surface – and dust generously with flour. Remove the dough from the fridge and divide into five equal portions. Using a rolling pin, roll each out until around ¼cm thick. Cut into long strips (around 10cm x 15cm) and once each one is rolled, layer on top of each other and cover with a damp cloth to stop it drying out. Cut as many as you can from the dough. Take any excess pastry, re-roll and repeat until you have used it all up.

Take a strip of dough and starting from the bottom right hand corner fold over to make a triangular shape leaving it to hang over the edge by 1cm. Then fold it onto itself maintaining a triangular shape and you will now have a nice little cone. Add 1½ tablespoons of the mixture to the cone and fold the remaining pastry. Once you get to the end, brush the edges with whisked egg and seal. Repeat this process until you have used up all the pastry.

Place a wok on a low to medium heat, add the vegetable oil and, once hot, add the samosas, a few at a time. It is important not to let the oil get too hot otherwise the outside of the samosa will cook too quickly. Fry until they are golden brown. Remove using a slotted spoon and drain on kitchen towel.

Turn the heat on the oil again and once hot, dip the cooked, drained samosas in the remaining egg and then the breadcrumbs ensuring an even coating and deep fry until golden brown in colour. Drain on kitchen roll and serve with a squeeze of lime.

SERVES: 4 PREP TIME: 25 COOKING TIME: 40 SPICE: 3/5

DEEP FRIED PATTIES

250g potatoes, peeled & diced
2 tbsp coconut oil
1 tsp black mustard seeds
1½ tsp cumin seeds
6 cloves of garlic, grated
2½ cm piece of ginger, grated
3 sprigs fresh curry leaves
1 leek, finely chopped
3 green chillies, finely chopped
10 shallots, finely chopped
1 red onion, finely chopped
1½ tsp roasted curry powder
½ level tsp chilli flakes
1½ tsp salt
½ tsp black pepper
500ml vegetable oil
juice of ½ a lime

FOR THE PASTRY

450g plain flour
juice ½ a lime
250ml warm water
1½ tsp salt
2 egg yolks
4 tbsp ghee

To prepare the dough for the pastry, take a large mixing bowl and sift in the flour then add the salt and ghee. Mix thoroughly by hand, squeezing the flour into the ghee until it becomes crumb-like. Squeeze in the lime juice and then add the water, a little at a time, mixing constantly (you may not need all the water, so see how it goes). Your mixture should now have a dough-like consistency. Ensure that there is no flour stuck to the bottom of the bowl, then dust your work surface with flour and knead for around 10 minutes until it is smooth and elastic. Wrap in cling film and place in the fridge for 1 hour.

Boil the potatoes in salted water for 10-15 minutes, or until soft. Drain and mash then set aside.

Place a large frying pan on a medium heat and add the coconut oil. Once sizzling, add the mustard seeds and once they start to spit, add the cumin seeds, garlic, ginger and curry leaves. Fry for 1 minute, then add the leeks, green chillies, shallots and onions and cook until the onions soften and turn golden brown. Add the curry powder, chilli flakes, salt and pepper to the pan, stir together and cook for another 2 minutes. Add the potatoes, and again mix until your fried veggies and spices are evenly distributed. Take off the heat and allow to cool for 10-15 minutes.

Take a chopping board – or use your kitchen surface – and dust generously with flour. Remove the dough from the fridge and divide into five equal portions. Using a rolling pin, roll out each out until around ¼ cm thick. Using a round pastry cutter (around 10cm diameter) cut as many discs as you can from the dough. Take any excess pastry, re-roll and repeat until you have used it all up.

Place 1-1½ tablespoons of the potato mixture on the centre of each disc, brush around the edges with a little egg yolk, and fold into a half moon shape. Then, using the back of a fork, press the edges together all the way around – as though you are crimping a pie. This will ensure a good seal so that the delicious filling does not escape. Repeat until you have used up all the pastry and mixture.

Place a wok on a low to medium heat, add the vegetable oil and, once hot, add the patties, a few at a time. I find it best to use a slotted metal spoon here as there is less chance of your patties splitting. Fry for 10 minutes, then turn up the heat and continue frying until they are golden brown. Remove using a slotted spoon and drain on kitchen towel.

SERVES: 4 PREP TIME: 30 COOKING TIME: 20 SPICE: 2/5

GREEN CHILLI COCONUT CHUTNEY

5 green chillies, roughly chopped
½ red onion, roughly chopped
2½ cm piece ginger, grated
4 cloves of garlic, grated
150g freshly grated coconut flesh
2 sprigs fresh curry leaves
3 tbsp coconut milk
juice of 1 lime
½ tsp salt
½ tsp black pepper

Add the chopped chilli, onion, ginger and garlic to a large pestle and mortar and grind to a smooth paste. Then add all the remaining ingredients and continue to grind until everything is combined and you are happy with the consistency. Personally, I like it a bit rough'n'ready but you can make it as smooth as you like.

Alternatively, if you own a food processor, you can just as easily throw it all in and blitz to a paste. Super easy and delicious too. Best served with warm Ulundu Vadai (see p92).

SERVES: 4 PREP TIME: 15 COOKING TIME: 0 SPICE: 4/5

BREADED FISH ROLLS

500ml coconut oil
150g potatoes, peeled & diced
500g salmon fillets
1½ tsp salt
½ tsp black pepper
25 shallots, finely chopped
10 green chillies, finely chopped
5 cloves of garlic, finely chopped
3 sprigs fresh curry leaves,
finely chopped
1 tsp black mustard seeds
1½ tsp cumin seeds
juice of 1 lime
4 eggs, whisked
half a loaf of bread,
(made into fine breadcrumbs)

FOR THE BATTER MIX
450g plain flour
1 tsp salt
1 egg
450ml cold water
300ml milk

To make the batter, add the flour and salt to a mixing bowl, then make a well in the centre and add the egg, water and milk. Whisk until smooth and without lumps.

Place a large frying pan on a medium heat with a dash of oil. Pour in the batter and tilt the pan to spread the mix to the edges. Cook on one side until the pancake is sturdy enough to remove from the pan in one piece. Repeat until you have 10 pancakes, then set these aside.

Boil the potatoes in salted water for 10-15 minutes, or until soft. Drain and mash then set aside.

Season the salmon fillets with salt and pepper. Place a large frying pan on a medium to high heat, and add a dash of vegetable oil. Once sizzling, add the salmon, skin side down. Cook for 3-4 minutes then, once the skin is crispy, turn the salmon over and fry for a further 2 minutes. Remove and break up into flakes. I love crispy salmon skin so I like to shred this too and add it to the mix but feel free to discard it.

Place the frying pan back on the heat and add a little more oil. Once sizzling, add the mustard seeds. Once they start to spit, add the cumin seeds together with all remaining ingredients (except the lime, eggs and bread) and fry until soft and slightly browned in colour. Allow to cool, then add the lime juice and the potato and mix everything together thoroughly by hand.

Take a pancake and place 2 tablespoons of the mixture 2½ cm from the bottom, then start to roll. Once you are halfway through rolling, fold the edges in on themselves, brush with egg yolk and continue to roll. When you get to the end, brush on a little more egg yolk and press together gently to seal your roll. Repeat this process until you have 10 rolls.

Place a wok on a high heat, add the remaining coconut oil and once hot, dip your rolls in the remaining whisked egg and then the breadcrumbs. Deep fry until golden brown. Drain on some kitchen towel and serve with a squeeze of lime.

SERVES: 4 PREP TIME: 35 COOKING TIME: 25 SPICE: 2/5

The Ocean

PERFECT WAVES, ALL TO YOURSELF

Surfing is a huge part of life for me and was the reason I went to Sri Lanka in the first place. The beautiful island is definitely an up and coming destination for surfers: it has great consistent waves and the perfectly clear turquoise water is insanely warm, almost like surfing in a bath! One of the most amazing things about the Sri Lankan ocean is that there are heaps of turtles, and you get to surf with them pretty much every day.

There are seasons on both the West and the East coasts, so you can surf the island all year round and the surf in Sri Lanka is perfect for both beginners and advanced surfers as there are such a wide range of spots. While the main hubs of Hikkaduwa (West) and Arugam Bay (East) become swamped in their high seasons, you can always hire your own little Tuk-Tuk and go exploring. If you look in the right places you can find some epic, completely deserted spots that are out of this world.

Whether you come for a short surf trip or a whole season, Sri Lanka is a must visit destination for all surfers. And if you like peaceful and un-crowded waves, go sooner rather than later!

Arugam Bay local shreading at
the main point.

CONSISTENT SURF ALL YEAR ROUND

There are loads of little surf shops around the island where you can rent boards, and of course some great bars where you can grab a few beers after a long day's surf.

Over the years I have left lots of my old boards at the guesthouse – the family rent them out and when I visit I also offer surf lessons to anyone who wants them. We met some kids at one of the secret spots that we used to surf; they were using old broken boards and even bits of wood, so every trip we leave some of our boards with them. They are really good kids and in return for the surfboards they took us diving for fish and crabs and cooked whatever we caught for dinner.

Each time I visit, they get better and better and although most of the initial group we met ten years ago have moved away, the younger generation are just as keen and still dive and surf everyday.

LIKE SURFING IN A BATH

The relaxed atmosphere of beach life in Sri Lanka is incredibly enticing. As a surfer and a lover of the ocean in general, the beach is where I spend most of my time. In addition to the amazing surf, there are tons of other water sports to get stuck in to: snorkeling and diving, peaceful canoeing trips along the rivers and lagoons, and white water rafting.

The colourful offshore coral reefs surrounding the island are home to the most beautiful, varied tropical creatures and there are also lots of old deep-sea wrecks to explore. Sri Lanka is a world-class destination for divers and snorkelers and many companies offer dive courses, but only a few are PADI certified, so be sure to check this beforehand.

Whale watching is synonymous with Sri Lanka and another incredible thing to do here. As well as the enormous, infamous blue whales, you can occasionally spot sperm whales too. With a huge continental shelf lying just off the south coast, it's an ideal habitat for these incredible specimens. Make sure you use a legitimate tour company who have the whales' best interests at heart, as it is important to look after these gentle giants.

Tropical Thunderstorm on the South Coast
during the monsoon season.

Seafood

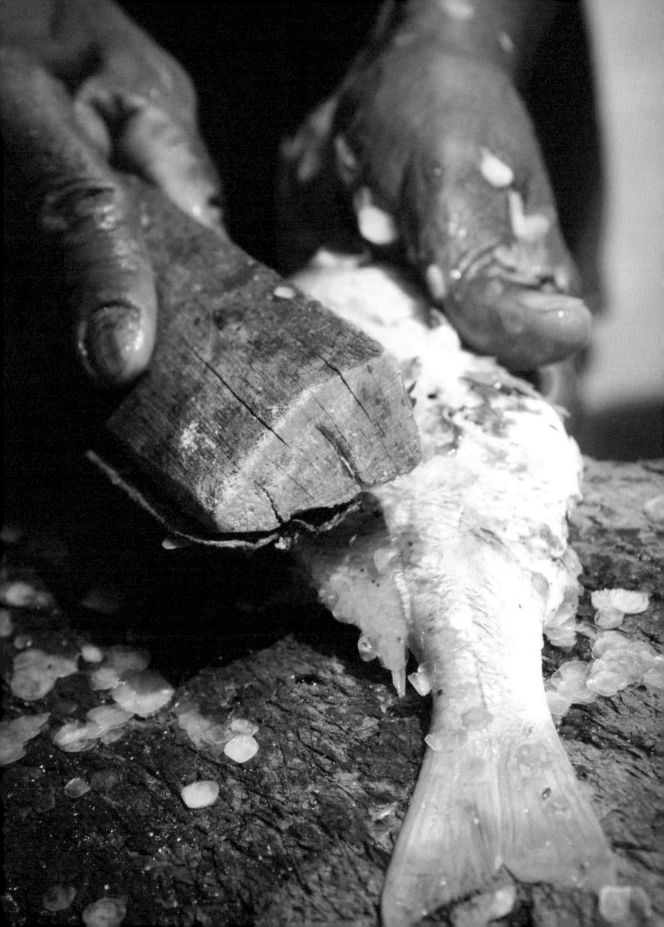

MALU, MALU, MALU
SRI LANKAN SEAFOOD

Seafood is an important source of protein in many diets around the world, especially in the coastal areas of Sri Lanka where fish often takes the place of meat, which is generally more expensive. In Sri Lanka, fish and seafood are as easy to come by as fruit and vegetables, and almost as inexpensive. Sri Lankans like to shop on a daily basis, ensuring that the produce they eat is as fresh as can be. As far as seafood is concerned, (unless it is preserved or dried) they almost always cook it on the day of purchase. This is easily done, as there are many fish vendors that deliver door to door; they travel on bicycles with boxes full of ice and fresh fish strapped to the back, crying out 'malu, malu, malu' (the Sinhalese word for fish) as they cycle past.

The seafood in Sri Lanka is extremely diverse and there is always plenty to choose from. I love to go down to the local harbour at sunrise, when the fishermen return with their night's catch. They lay it out and the loud hustle of the bartering begins. Although you have to pay a small fee to enter the harbour area, the price of produce is somewhat cheaper than that in the main markets. It also helps to know the locals as you will always get a fair price.

When shopping in the UK, whether at your local fishmongers or a supermarket, make sure the seafood you buy is MSC certified and sustainable. Check msc.org if you are unsure.

RANJI'S MACKERAL CURRY

400g deboned mackerel fillets
4 tbsp coconut oil
½ tsp black mustard seeds
1 tsp cumin seeds
3 tsp roasted curry powder
8 cloves of garlic, grated
1 red onion, roughly chopped
2 fresh tomatoes, quartered
2 capsicums, quartered
½ cinnamon stick
2 sprigs fresh curry leaves
1 x 400ml tin of coconut milk
100ml fish stock
juice of ½ a lime
1 tsp salt
1 tsp black pepper
a handful of fresh coriander

Take a frying pan and place on a medium to high heat, then add half the coconut oil. Once sizzling, add the mackerel, skin side down.

Cook for 2-3 minutes until the skin has crisped up nicely. Turn over and fry for another minute. Take out and place on a chopping board.

Place the pan back on a medium to high heat and add the remaining coconut oil. When sizzling, add the mustard seeds. Once they start to spit, add the cumin seeds and curry powder. Fry for 1 minute then add the garlic, onion, tomatoes and capsicums. Fry for another couple of minutes, stirring.

Add the mackerel to the pan with all the remaining ingredients except the lime juice and cook on a medium heat for 10-15 minutes or until the oil starts to separate. The cooking time really depends on the size of your fish. Check regularly and when the fish begins to flake apart, it's done.

Take off the heat and leave to cool for 2 minutes. Then add in the lime juice. Season to taste and finish with a handful of coriander leaves, if using, then serve.

SERVES: 4 PREP TIME: 15 COOKING TIME: 20 SPICE: 2/5

BREADED FISH CUTLETS

4 large potatoes (400g),
(peeled & diced)
400g salmon fillet,
(skinned and cut into
2½ cm chunks)
250ml vegetable oil
½ tsp black mustard seeds
1 tsp cumin seeds
6 sprigs fresh curry leaves,
finely chopped
6 fresh green chillies, chopped
1 red onion, finely chopped
15 shallots, diced
6 cloves of garlic, grated
½ tsp roasted curry powder
1½ tsp salt
1 tsp black pepper
juice of 1 lime
4 eggs, whisked
500g breadcrumbs
lime wedges, to serve

Boil the potatoes in salted water for 10-15 minutes, or until soft. Remove with a slotted spoon, reserving the cooking water, and roughly mash.

Place the salmon in the potato cooking water and boil for 3-4 minutes, or until it begins to flake apart. Drain on kitchen towel, then place in a large mixing bowl and break up using the back of a fork. Add the salmon to the mashed potatoes, mix together thoroughly and set aside.

Place a frying pan on a medium heat and add 3 tablespoons of vegetable oil. Once sizzling, add the mustard seeds. Once they begin to spit, add the cumin seeds, curry leaves, green chillies, onion, shallots, garlic and remaining seasoning. Stir until evenly distributed. Take off the heat and allow to cool for around 20 minutes before adding the mixture to the fish and potatoes. Squeeze in the lime juice and again mix together well.

Roll the mixture into golf ball-sized pieces and repeat until you have used it all up. Dip the balls into the whisked egg, then the breadcrumbs. Repeat this process until all the balls are breaded.

Add the remaining vegetable oil to a wok and place on a medium to high heat. Once sizzling, fry the balls, a few at a time, until golden brown. Drain on kitchen towel and serve with a wedge of lime.

SERVES: 4 PREP TIME: 30 COOKING TIME: 30 SPICE: 2/5

USEFUL TIP: As with the fish rolls, you can add a few teaspoons of prawn extract to your mixture, which will give these little balls a much deeper flavour.

BIRANGA'S CRAB CURRY

4 medium sized crabs
1½ tsp curry powder
1½ level tsp chilli powder
1½ tsp turmeric powder
1 tsp English mustard
3 tbsp coconut oil
½ tsp black mustard seeds
1 tsp cumin seeds
6 cloves of garlic, grated
4 fresh green chillies,
roughly chopped
4 sprigs fresh curry leaves
2 red onions, finely chopped
2 cardamom pods
1 tsp roasted fenugreek seeds,
crushed
1 cinnamon stick
200ml water
2 fresh tomatoes, diced
½ x 400g tin of chopped tomatoes
2 tsp salt
1 tsp black pepper
1 x 400ml tin of coconut milk
a handful of fresh coriander
(optional)

As far as I know, the most humane and painless way to kill crabs is to freeze them for at least 2 hours before use. Once frozen, place in cool water to defrost (around 25 minutes). Once defrosted, they need to be cleaned and quartered ready for cooking.

Place the crabs on a chopping board or kitchen surface belly side up. Pull off the triangular-shaped belly flaps. Next, turn them over and remove the shell by inserting your thumb between the body and the shell at the rear of each crab and pulling its shell upwards. Inside you will see the spongy gills – they look a bit like withered fingers. These are not for eating and need to be removed. Wash the crabs thoroughly under running water then, using a heavy knife or cleaver, cut in half lengthwise and then into quarters. You are now ready to start cooking.

Take a large mixing bowl and place your quartered crabs inside. Add 1 teaspoon of curry powder, 1 teaspoon of chilli powder, 1 teaspoon of turmeric powder and all the mustard. Mix together thoroughly by hand, ensuring that all parts of the crabs are evenly coated.

Place a large saucepan on a medium heat and add the coconut oil. Once sizzling, first add the mustard and cumin seeds. Once the mustard seeds start to pop throw in the garlic, chillies, curry leaves and onions and fry for 2-3 minutes. Then add the remaining curry, chilli and turmeric powders, cardamom pods and roasted fenugreek seeds together with the cinnamon stick. Stir constantly until it turns into a paste. Add the crab quarters to the pot and stir until they are evenly coated in the paste. There should be some spice mix left in the mixing bowl used for the crabs: add 200ml of water to this and stir together, making sure all spices are combined with the water, then add to the pot. Finally add both the fresh and tinned tomatoes.

Now add the salt and pepper, turn to a medium to high heat and cover. Check regularly and, when the stock has reduced by half, add the coconut milk. Cover again, and cook for another 3-4 minutes or until the oil starts to separate, then take off the heat.

At this point, you can drain the sauce and blend in a food processor – I find it helps the flavours to infuse and gives the sauce more depth.

Season to taste and finish with a handful of coriander leaves.

SERVES: 4 PREP TIME: 40 COOKING TIME: 20 SPICE: 3/5

JAYANTHA'S PRAWN CURRY

2 tbsp coconut oil
2 fresh green chillies,
roughly chopped
8 cloves of garlic, grated
2 red onions, finely chopped
2 fresh tomatoes, diced
25-30 raw unshelled prawns
2 sprigs fresh curry leaves
2 tsp curry powder
½ tsp roasted curry powder
½ tsp turmeric powder
1½ level tsp chilli powder
250ml fish stock
1 x 400ml tin of coconut milk
juice of ½ a lime
1 tsp salt
1 tsp black pepper
a handful of fresh coriander

Place a wok on a medium to high heat and add the coconut oil.

Once sizzling, add the chillies, garlic, onions and tomatoes. Fry for 3-4 minutes, stirring occasionally. Then add the prawns.

Turn down to a medium heat, then add the curry leaves, curry powders, turmeric, chilli powder, coriander, stock or water and coconut milk. Bring to the boil.

When the oil starts to separate, take off the heat and leave to cool for 2 minutes, then squeeze in the lime juice.

Season to taste and finish with a handful of coriander leaves, if using, then serve.

SERVES: 4 PREP TIME: 15 COOKING TIME: 10 SPICE: 3/5

USEFUL TIP: Add a little prawn extract powder to make it even more tasty. (See tip on Anoma's Prawn Curry, p146.)

DEVILLED FISH STIR FRY

400g tuna steaks,
cut into 2½cm chunks
250ml water
juice of 1 lime
1 tsp salt
2 tsp black pepper
500ml coconut oil
2 tbsp vegetable oil
1 bulb of garlic, grated
5 fresh green chillies, chopped
4 red onions, roughly chopped
1 leek, roughly chopped
5 capsicums, roughly chopped
4 fresh tomatoes, diced
2 level tsp chilli powder
2 tsp soy sauce
2 tbsp tomato puree
2 tbsp oyster sauce

FOR THE GORAKA PASTE:
6 pieces goraka
125ml water
½ teaspoon salt

Add the goraka and water to a small saucepan and bring to the boil. Decant into a pestle and mortar along with the salt and grind to a paste. Set aside.

Put the tuna, water, lime juice, goraka paste, and the salt and pepper in a large saucepan. Mix together thoroughly and place on a medium to high heat until it boils dry. This should take 5-10 minutes but keep an eye on it as you don't want to burn the fish.

Place a wok on a high heat and add the coconut oil. Once sizzling, add the chunks of fish one at a time. Fry until golden brown in colour then remove and leave to drain on kitchen towel.

Lastly, place a large frying pan or wok on a medium heat and add 2 tablespoons of vegetable oil. Once sizzling, add the garlic. Cook for a minute then add the chillies and the rest of the vegetables, apart from the tomatoes. After 5 minutes, add the fish, tomatoes, chilli powder, soy sauce, tomato puree and oyster sauce. Stir thoroughly.

Continue cooking on a medium heat for 3 minutes and then serve.

SERVES: 4 PREP TIME: 25 COOKING TIME: 35 SPICE: 4/5

MALU AMBUL THIAL

8 pieces goraka
125ml water
3 tbsp salt
3 tbsp black pepper
500g fish of your choice

Add the goraka and water to a small saucepan and bring to the boil. Decant into a pestle and mortar along with the salt and pepper and grind to a paste. Set aside.

Cut the fish into 2½ cm chunks and smother with paste, making sure that they are evenly coated.

Add to a medium sized saucepan on a low heat and cook for around 10-12 minutes, or until the fish starts to flake apart.

Season to taste and serve.

SERVES: 4 PREP TIME: 5 COOKING TIME: 15 SPICE: 1/5

USEFUL FACT: This dish can be prepared with any type of fish and is renowned throughout Sri Lanka. It is probably the easiest recipe in this book! Don't let this put you off, as it is super tasty and especially great served with other curried dishes. As with most dishes, it tastes better when cooked in a clay pot.

ANOMA'S PRAWN CURRY

3 tbsp coconut oil
20-25 large raw unshelled prawns
½ tsp black mustard seeds
1 tsp cumin seeds
1 tsp roasted fenugreek seeds,
1 sprig fresh curry leaves
1 tsp roasted curry powder
¼ tsp turmeric powder
½ cinnamon stick
10cm piece rampe (pandan leaf)
5-6 fresh green chillies,
roughly chopped
2 fresh tomatoes, diced
2 x 400ml tins of coconut milk
juice of ¾ of a lime
1 tsp salt
1 tsp black pepper
a handful of fresh coriander
(optional)

Place a wok on a high heat and add the coconut oil. Once sizzling, flash-fry your prawns for 1-2 minutes until coloured nicely. This extra cooking stage will give the finished dish a deeper flavour.

Add all the remaining ingredients except the coconut milk and lime juice to the wok and stir together thoroughly, ensuring the prawns are evenly coated. Cook on a medium heat for 10 minutes. Add the coconut milk (and prawn extract, if using – see below) and continue cooking for a further 5 minutes, or until the oil starts to separate.

Take off the heat, allow to cool slightly, add in the lime juice and stir to combine. Season to taste and finish with a handful of coriander leaves, if using, then serve.

SERVES: 4 PREP TIME: 10 COOKING TIME: 20 SPICE: 2/5

USEFUL TIP: I tend to leave the prawns intact but you can add extra flavour to this dish by de-heading and peeling the prawns after flash frying them and making what is known as prawn extract. Simply slow roast the prawn heads and tails, then crush them up into a powder. Prawn extract can also be stored in an airtight container for up to three months and added to any fish curry to enhance its flavour.

THE ULTIMATE SEAFOOD BBQ

THE ULTIMATE SEAFOOD BBQ WITH RASIKA

(The Sri Lankan Rastaman)

This is Rasika: he's a good friend of mine and an incredible cook. Rasika was getting a bus back from town one day when he saw me and some friends on the side of the road, surfboards in hand. He came up and told us about his little guesthouse, 'Uprising'. It is a stone's throw away from some of the best waves I have ever ridden – I can't wait to get back there.

The guesthouse is a quiet shanti – there are pictures of Bob Marley everywhere and Buddhist flags hanging between the trees. Rasika is a super mellow yet very eccentric guy. He is as enthusiastic about cooking as I am, which is quite unusual in Sri Lankan culture as traditionally it's the women who rule in the kitchen, and it is rare to find men who like cooking.

When I go and stay with Rasika all we do is cook, listen to reggae, go surfing and play carrom, the local game. We visit the local markets in the morning to get the ingredients for the day. There is always heaps of amazing and unusual produce, all fresh and ridiculously cheap. Rasika doesn't eat meat so we mainly buy fish and vegetables but he is a really creative cook and everything he makes tastes amazingly good.

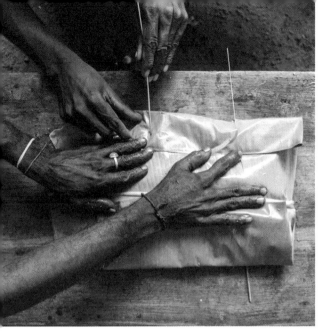

COOKING WITH INSTINCTS

After we come back from the markets we go back to the guesthouse, crack open a beer, put some reggae on and start cooking. Rasika has all of his spices in little bowls, bags or old jam jars he's found – not like the UK where we have all our jars neatly stacked in a spice rack. Rasika's spices aren't labelled either – he knows what they are and just adds what he feels like, cooking with his instincts. My favourite meal that we cooked together – and the one that reminds me of Rasika the most – is the big seafood BBQ.

We fired up the BBQ, wrapped up all the beautiful fresh fish in dampened banana leaves, along with a load of spices, and kicked back until it was done. It was so simple, but honestly one of the tastiest meals I've had.

CRISPY FRIED SQUID CURRY

500g fresh squid
plain flour, to dust
1½ tsp salt
1 tsp black pepper
4 tbsp coconut oil
1 tsp black mustard seeds
1 tsp cumin seeds
¼ tsp fenugreek seeds
1 sprig curry leaves
7½ cm piece rampe (pandan leaf)
½ tsp coriander powder
1 tsp curry powder
¼ tsp turmeric powder
½ cinnamon stick
4-5 fresh green chillies, chopped
6 cloves of garlic, grated
5 shallots, roughly chopped
1 red onion, roughly chopped
2 tomatoes, quartered
2 x 400ml tins of coconut milk
juice of ½ a lime
500ml vegetable oil

You can ask your fishmonger to prepare your squid. To do it yourself, first separate the bodies of the squid from the tentacles, then remove the black beak in the centre of the tentacles and discard it. Next, place your hand into the body of the squid and remove the plastic-like back bone. Take out the innards and discard. Finally, place a large knife into the cleaned squid body and cut it in half, then repeat on the other side.

Score the inside of each piece of squid with a diamond pattern, being careful not to cut all the way through the flesh. Add the scored squid to the tentacles, pat it all dry, then dust with a little flour and seasoning and set aside ready for deep frying.

Place a wok or high sided frying pan on a medium heat and add the coconut oil. Once sizzling, add the mustard seeds. Once they start to spit, add the cumin seeds and the rest of the ingredients (except the coconut milk, lime and vegetable oil) and mix thoroughly.

Cook for 10 minutes, or until the oil starts to separate, stirring occasionally. Add the coconut milk and reduce the heat to low before cooking for 5 more minutes. Take off the heat, allow to cool slightly, then add the lime juice, stir thoroughly and set aside.

In a separate pan, add the vegetable oil. Once sizzling hot, add the squid and fry for a couple of minutes until golden brown, then remove and leave to drain on some kitchen towel. Serve up the curry and place the deep fried squid on top. Season to taste and serve.

SERVES: 4 PREP TIME: 20 COOKING TIME: 20 SPICE: 2/5

YELLOW FISH CURRY

2 tbsp coconut oil
500g tuna steaks,
(cut into 2½ cm chunks)
½ tsp salt
½ tsp black pepper
½ tsp black mustard seeds
½ tsp roasted curry powder
1 tsp cumin seeds
1½ tsp turmeric powder
½ level tsp chilli powder
3 pieces goraka
(soaked in hot water for
20 minutes)
1 cinnamon stick
4 capsicums, quartered
2 tomatoes, quartered
6 fresh green chillies, chopped
2 sprigs fresh curry leaves
2 small red onions, chopped
1 x 400ml tin of coconut milk
a handful of fresh coriander
(optional)

Place a large frying pan on a medium heat and add the coconut oil. Once sizzling, add the tuna chunks together with the salt and pepper. Fry for around 2-3 minutes until the tuna starts to colour slightly, then take off the heat.

Add all the remaining ingredients (apart from half the coconut milk) to a large saucepan and stir together. Simmer on a low heat for 10 minutes, stirring occasionally.

Add the remaining 200ml coconut milk and simmer for 5 more minutes, or until the oil starts to separate. Season to taste and finish with a handful of coriander leaves, if using, then serve.

SERVES: 4 PREP TIME: 10 COOKING TIME: 20 SPICE: 3/5

GAYANI'S FISH CURRY

500g skin on salmon fillets,
(cut into 2½ cm chunks)
1 tsp salt
½ tsp black pepper
½ tsp turmeric powder
1 tbsp coconut oil
½ tsp black mustard seeds
½ tsp cumin seeds
7½ cm piece of rampe
(pandan leaf)
1 sprig fresh curry leaves
3 cloves of garlic, grated
2 fresh green chillies, chopped
1 red onion, finely chopped
1 x 400ml tin of coconut milk
1 piece of goraka
(soaked in hot water for
20 minutes)
3 tsp roasted curry powder
½ level tsp chilli powder
½ tsp roasted fenugreek seeds
(crushed)
1 stick cinnamon

On a chopping board, season the salmon pieces with salt, pepper and turmeric powder. Mix together by hand, making sure each piece is evenly coated.

Place a large high-sided frying pan on a medium to high heat and add half of the coconut oil. Once sizzling, add the mustard seeds, cumin seeds, rampe and curry leaves. Cook for 30 seconds, then add the garlic, green chillies and red onion. Fry until the onion starts to soften and turn golden in colour.

Push the fried ingredients to one side of the pan and add the rest of the coconut oil. Once sizzling, add the salmon to the pan, skin side down. Cook for 2-3 minutes or until the skin has crisped up nicely, then carefully mix together with a wooden spoon, being careful not to break apart the fish.

Add the coconut milk, goraka and curry powder. Reduce the heat to low and gently stir. Cook for 4 minutes, then add the chilli powder, roasted fenugreek seeds and cinnamon. Cook for a couple more minutes, or until the oil starts to separate.

Season to taste and serve.

SERVES: 4 PREP TIME: 25 COOKING TIME: 15 SPICE: 2/5

KINGFISH CURRY

3 tsp chilli flakes
1 tbsp black peppercorns
2 tsp roasted curry powder
2 cloves of garlic, grated
3 tbsp coconut oil
4 red onions, roughly chopped
4 fresh green chillies, chopped
500g king fish or tuna,
(cut into 2½ cm chunks)
1 sprig fresh curry leaves
10cm piece of rampe
(pandan leaf)
½ tsp cumin seeds
1 level tsp chilli powder
½ a cinnamon stick
500ml fish stock or water
1 x 400ml tin of coconut milk
4 pieces of goraka,
(soaked in hot water for
20 minutes)
4 fresh tomatoes, quartered
2 tsp salt
a handful of fresh coriander
(optional)

Place a frying pan on a medium heat and dry roast the chilli flakes, peppercorns and curry powder.

Add to a pestle and mortar with the garlic and 2 tablespoons of water and grind to make a paste.

Place a large frying pan on a medium to high heat and add the coconut oil. Once sizzling, add the spicy garlic paste, onions, green chillies and fish.

Fry for 3-4 minutes until the onions start to soften and colour nicely, then remove from the heat and add the curry leaves, rampe, cumin, chilli, cinnamon and coriander.

Stir thoroughly, add the stock and place on a low to medium heat for 10-12 minutes.

Finally add the coconut milk, tomatoes and goraka and simmer for 5 minutes, or until the oil starts to separate.

Season to taste and finish with a handful of coriander leaves, if using, then serve.

SERVES: 4 PREP TIME: 15 COOKING TIME: 20 SPICE: 4/5

SEER FISH WHITE CURRY

500g mackerel fillets,
(cut into 2½ cm chunks)
3 cloves of garlic, grated
4-5 fresh green chillies, chopped
5 shallots, finely chopped
2 fresh tomatoes, diced
1 sprig fresh curry leaves
1 tsp curry powder
½ tsp roasted fenugreek seeds,
(crushed)
¼ tsp turmeric
½ cinnamon stick
7½ cm piece of rampe
(pandan leaf)
3 pieces goraka (soaked in
hot water for 20 minutes)
1 x 400ml tin of coconut milk
juice of ½ a lime
1½ tsp salt
1 tsp black pepper
a handful of fresh coriander
(optional)

Add all the ingredients except the coconut milk, lime juice, seasoning and coriander to a saucepan and mix together.

Place on a medium heat and cook for 10 minutes, stirring occasionally. Add the coconut milk, reduce the heat to low and cook for 5 more minutes, or until the oil starts to separate.

Take off the heat and allow to cool slightly, then add the lime juice and stir to mix.

Season to taste and finish with a handful of coriander leaves, if using, then serve.

SERVES: 4 PREP TIME: 15 COOKING TIME: 15 SPICE: 2/5

USEFUL FACT: Seer is also referred to as 'King Mackerel' in some areas of Sri Lanka. If you are unable to find it then fresh mackerel is a great substitute. This recipe is definitely one of my favourites!

Off to Market

THE BUSTLING MARKETS OF SRI LANKA

The bustling markets of Sri Lanka offer a wide variety of fresh seasonal produce all year round. They range from one-man street vendors with their fruit and veg laid out on hessian floor mats, to huge weekly markets with hundreds of stalls. These markets offer a variety of goods, including aromatic spices, the freshest seafood, delicious fruit and vegetables, sweet treats, natural oils, and so much more.

Spices such as cinnamon, cloves, cardamom, nutmeg and pepper are found in abundance on the island, together with the tastiest blends of curry powders I have ever come across. These markets really indulge your senses with their tantalizing aromas and array of colourful produce. The hustle and bustle is exciting: sellers shout out prices per gram, weigh their produce in battered old brass scales, and bargain with hordes of housewives – and they never stop smiling.

As far as money is concerned, you will be amazed by what you can get for your budget. As with most items in Sri Lanka, the price is always negotiable and bargaining is part of the culture. Have fun with it but try to remember that no matter how much something costs, you are probably arguing over a few pence, so try not to take it too seriously.

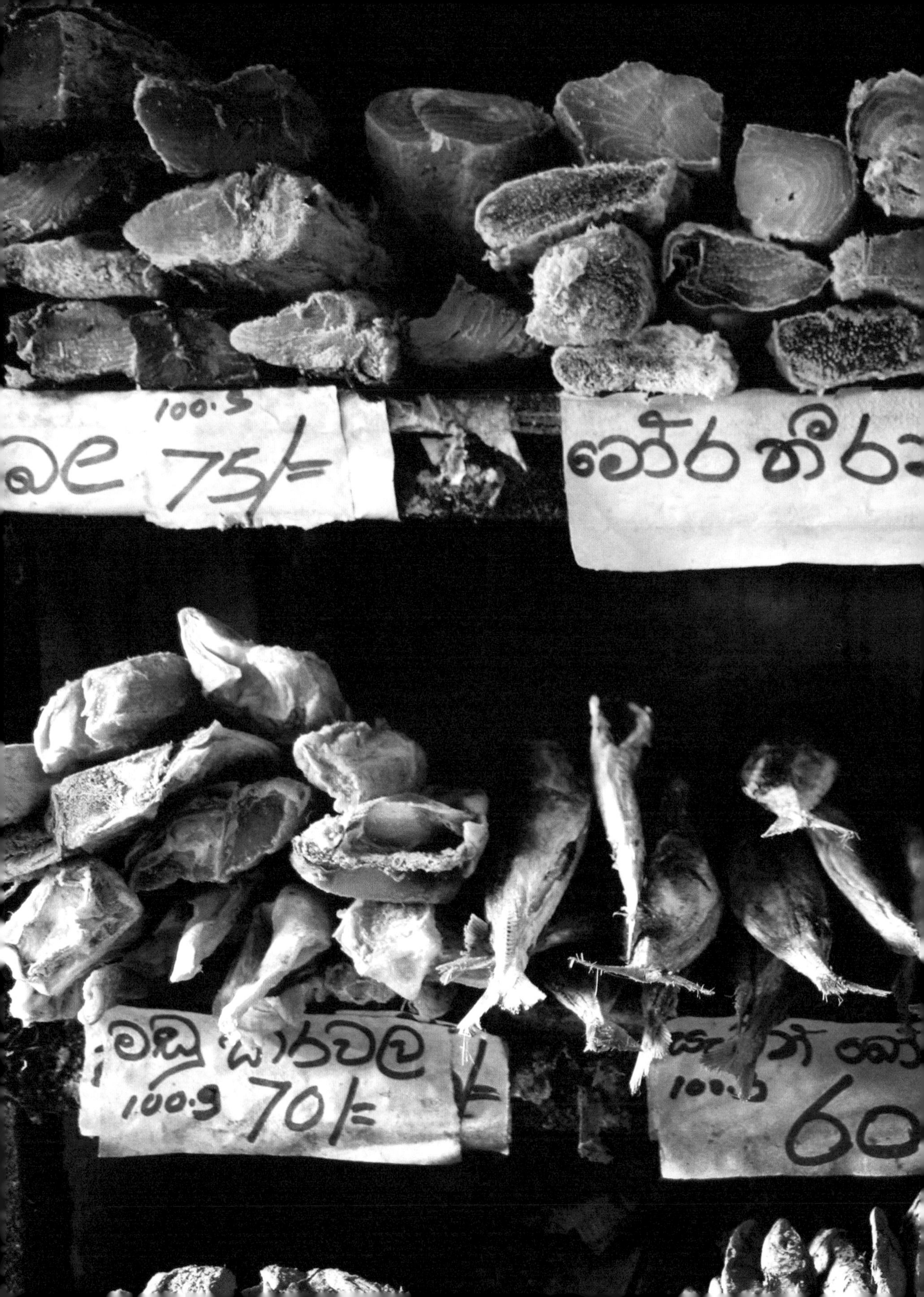
75/=
70/=

90/=

කට්ටා   රු.100.

100/=

Veggie Dishes

DEEP FRIED EGG CURRY

6 eggs
3 tbsp coconut oil
3 cloves of garlic, grated
7½ cm piece of ginger, grated
3 fresh green chillies, chopped
1 Bombay (white) onion, chopped
3 sprigs fresh curry leaves
2 tsp roasted curry powder
2 tsp ground coriander
5cm piece (½ stick) cinnamon
2 cloves, crushed
2 cardamom pods, crushed
3 pieces goraka
(soaked in hot water for
20 minutes)
1 level tsp chilli flakes
1 tsp turmeric powder
1 x 400ml tin of coconut milk
500ml vegetable oil
1 tsp salt
1 tsp black pepper

Place a large saucepan of cold salted water on a high heat and add the eggs. Once the water is boiling, continue to cook for 1 minute, then take off the heat and set aside to cool fully before peeling.

Add the coconut oil to a large, high-sided frying pan and put on a medium to high heat. Once sizzling, add the garlic, ginger, chillies, onions and curry leaves. Fry for 2-3 minutes or until the onions start to soften and turn golden.

Add this mixture and all the remaining ingredients (except the vegetable oil) to a large saucepan. Cover and cook on a medium heat for 10 minutes, or until the oil starts to separate.

Add vegetable oil to a wok and place on a medium to high heat. When it is sizzling, add the eggs and fry until golden brown – this should only take a minute or two.

Cut the eggs in half, then add to the curry. Season to taste and serve.

SERVES: 4 PREP TIME: 30 COOKING TIME: 25 SPICE: 2/5

FRIED POTATO CURRY
With Crispy Bombay Onions

750ml water
250ml vegetable oil
500g potatoes, roughly chopped
2 Bombay (white) onions, chopped
4 fresh green chillies, chopped
½ tsp roasted curry powder
¼ tsp turmeric powder
2 tsp of Maldive fish flakes
(optional)
1 sprig fresh curry leaves
½ cinnamon stick
1 tsp salt
2 x 400ml tins of coconut milk
juice of 1 lime
a handful of fresh coriander
(optional)

Place a large saucepan on a high heat and add the potatoes together with 750ml of water. Par-boil for around 10 minutes the take out and set aside.Next place a wok on a high heat and add the vegetable oil. Once sizzling, add the potatoes and fry until crispy, stirring occasionally. Once they turn golden brown, carefully remove with a slotted spoon and leave to drain on kitchen towel.

In the same pan, fry the onions, again until golden. Remove with a slotted spoon and leave to drain on kitchen towel to remove any excess oil.

Place the remaining ingredients (except 200ml coconut milk and the lime juice) in a medium sized saucepan. Bring to the boil and then reduce the heat to low.

Add the reserved coconut milk and lime juice to the pan and simmer for 10 minutes, or until the oil starts to separate. Remove from the heat and add the crispy potatoes and onions.

Season to taste and finish with a handful of coriander leaves, if using, then serve.

SERVES: 4 PREP TIME: 20 COOKING TIME: 25 SPICE: 2/5

USEFUL FACT: I love this dish and eat it as often as I can. It adds a different textural element to the meal when eaten with other traditional Sri Lankan curries.

EAST COAST PUMPKIN CURRY

2 tbsp coconut oil
2 tsp black mustard seeds
2 tsp cumin seeds
4 cloves of garlic, grated
4 green chillies, finely chopped
2 red onions, roughly chopped
1 tsp curry powder
1 tsp salt
3 sprigs fresh curry leaves
7½ cm piece rampe
(pandan leaf)
1 level tsp chilli flakes
1 tsp roasted fenugreek seeds,
(crushed)
½ stick cinnamon
½ tsp turmeric powder
½ tsp sugar
1 tsp black pepper
500g pumpkin, (deseeded
and cut into 2½ cm cubes)
1 x 400ml tin of coconut milk
Juice of ½ a lime

Place a large high-sided frying pan on a medium to high heat and add the coconut oil. Once sizzling, add the mustard seeds.

When they start to spit, add the cumin seeds, garlic, chillies, onions, curry powder, salt and curry leaves.

Fry for 3-4 minutes, or until the onions start to soften and turn golden in colour, then add all the remaining ingredients (except the lime juice) cover, and cook on a medium heat for 15 minutes, or until the oil starts to separate.

Allow to cool slightly, then add the lime juice and mix together. Season to taste, and serve.

SERVES: 4 PREP TIME: 30 COOKING TIME: 20 SPICE: 3/5

GAYANI'S SWEET POTATO CURRY

4 tbsp coconut oil
1 sprig fresh curry leaves
5 shallots, roughly chopped
2 fresh green chillies, chopped
1 clove of garlic, grated
450g sweet potato
(cut into 2½ cm cubes)
2½ cm piece rampe
(pandan leaf)
1½ tsp roasted curry powder
¼ tsp roasted fenugreek seeds
(crushed)
2 x 400ml tins of coconut milk
1 tsp salt
1 tsp black pepper

Place a large frying pan on a high heat with a dash of oil and add the curry leaves, shallots, chillies and garlic.

Fry for around 3-4 minutes then add the sweet potato along with all the remaining ingredients.

Cover and cook for 15 minutes, or until the sweet potato is cooked but still slightly al dente.

Take off the lid and cook uncovered for 5 minutes, or until the oil starts to separate, then remove from the heat.

Season to taste and serve.

SERVES: 4 PREP TIME: 10 COOKING TIME: 20 SPICE: 2/5

RANJI'S BRINGAL CURRY

500g brinjal (aubergine)
2 tbsp coconut oil
1 tsp black mustard seeds
3 sprigs fresh curry leaves
3 fresh green chillies, chopped
1 small red onion, chopped
1 tsp black pepper
1 tsp chilli powder
1 cinnamon stick
2 tsp curry powder
½ tsp dill seeds
7½ cm piece rampe
(pandan leaf)
1½ tsp salt
1 x 400ml tin of coconut milk

To prepare the aubergine, cut off the top and bottom using a sharp knife, then cut in half lengthways and into quarters (again lengthways). Cut into strips.

Place a large high-sided frying pan on a medium to high heat and add the coconut oil. Once sizzling, add the mustard seeds and curry leaves. When the mustard seeds start to pop, add the chillies and red onion. Fry for 2-3 minutes, or until the onions start to soften and turn golden.

Add the mixture to a large saucepan along with the aubergine and remaining ingredients. Mix together thoroughly and cook on a low heat for 10-12 minutes.

Season to taste and serve.

SERVES: 4 PREP TIME: 10 COOKING TIME: 15 SPICE: 3/5

USEFUL FACT: Brinjal (or aubergine as it is more commonly known in the western world), is a very low calorie vegetable. It contains large amounts of B-complex vitamins which are essential for amino acid metabolism and boosting energy levels within the body.

WEST COAST BEETROOT CURRY

3 tbsp coconut oil
2 sprigs fresh curry leaves
1½ Bombay (white) onions,
(chopped)
2 fresh green chillies, chopped
500g beetroot,
(peeled and chopped into
thin strips)
2 level tsp chilli powder
2 tsp ground coriander
1 tsp sugar
3 tsp vinegar
1½ tsp salt
1 tsp black pepper
1 x 400ml tin of coconut milk
a handful of fresh coriander
(optional)

Place a medium sized saucepan on a medium heat and add the coconut oil. Once sizzling, add the curry leaves, onions and chillies and fry for 2 minutes.

Add the strips of beetroot and all the remaining ingredients (except the coconut milk) and continue frying for another couple of minutes.

Add the coconut milk and simmer on a low heat for 15-20 minutes, or until the oil starts to separate. Season to taste and finish with a handful of coriander leaves, if using, then serve.

SERVES: 4 PREP TIME: 15 COOKING TIME: 25 SPICE: 4/5

USEFUL FACT: Beetroot gets its distinct red colour from betalain antioxidant pigments. These nutrients have been shown to provide antioxidant, anti-inflammatory and detoxification support to the body.

ANOMA'S POTATO CURRY

500g potatoes,
(peeled and chopped into
2½ cm cubes)
6 fresh green chillies, chopped
6 shallots, roughly chopped
9cm piece rampe (pandan leaf)
2 sprigs fresh curry leaves
¼ tsp turmeric powder
¼ tsp roasted fenugreek seeds
(crushed)
½ tsp curry powder
½ cinnamon stick
2 x 400ml tins of coconut milk
1 tsp salt
1 tsp black pepper
juice of ½ a lime
a handful of fresh coriander
(optional)

Boil the potatoes in salted water for 10 minutes then drain.

Place a large saucepan on a medium heat and add half the coconut milk together with the potatoes and other ingredients (except the lime juice).

Cook for 7-8 minutes, stirring occasionally to stop the coconut milk from congealing.

Add the reserved coconut milk and simmer until the potatoes are fully cooked and the oil starts to separate.

Take off the heat and allow to cool slightly before adding the lime juice. Season to taste and finish with a handful of coriander leaves, if using, then serve.

SERVES: 4 PREP TIME: 15 COOKING TIME: 20 SPICE: 2/5

Dried red chillies, used in a variety of dishes on the island

SOUTHERN CASHEW NUT CURRY

250g raw cashew nuts
1½ tsp salt
¼ tsp turmeric powder
1 tbsp curry powder
2 pieces goraka
(soaked in hot water for
20 minutes)
3 tbsp coconut oil
10cm piece rampe
(pandan leaf)
1 sprig fresh curry leaves
1 Bombay (white) onion, chopped
2 fresh green chillies, chopped
2 cloves of garlic, crushed
2½ cm piece ginger, grated
½ cinnamon stick
1 x 400ml tin of coconut milk
1½ tsp black pepper
a handful of fresh coriander
(optional)

Boil the kettle. Place the cashews in a bowl and add enough boiling water to cover them. Cover with a lid or clean tea towel and leave to soak for around 30 minutes.

Drain thoroughly then add the salt, turmeric, curry powder and goraka. Mix together thoroughly until the cashews are all evenly coated.

Heat the coconut oil in a medium sized saucepan. Once sizzling, add the rampe and curry leaves and fry for 30 seconds before adding the onion, green chillies, garlic, ginger and cinnamon. Fry until the onion is soft and golden brown. Add the cashews and stir until they are well coated, then add half (200ml) of the coconut milk. Cover and simmer on a low heat until the cashews are soft.

Add the remaining coconut milk and bring to the boil slowly on a low heat, then leave to rest for around 10 minutes.

Season to taste and finish with a handful of coriander leaves, if using, then serve.

SERVES: 4 PREP TIME: 45 COOKING TIME: 20 SPICE: 2/5

USEFUL FACT: Cashew nuts are a very rich source of minerals, especially potassium, copper, iron, magnesium and zinc, which are concentrated in the nuts.

WEST COAST PUMPKIN CURRY

4 tbsp coconut oil
1 tsp black mustard seeds
8 cloves of garlic, grated
2 fresh green chillies, chopped
4 shallots, roughly chopped
2 red onions, roughly chopped
3 sprigs fresh curry leaves
500g pumpkin,
(deseeded and cut into
2½ cm cubes)
1 cinnamon stick
1 tsp ground coriander
3 pieces goraka
(soaked in hot water for
20 minutes)
2 tsp roasted curry powder
100g roasted ground coconut
2 x 400ml tins of coconut milk
1½ tsp salt
½ tsp black pepper
a handful of fresh coriander
(optional)

Take a large, high-sided frying pan and add the coconut oil. Once sizzling, add the mustard seeds. As soon as they start to spit, add the garlic, chillies, shallots, onions and curry leaves to the pan.

Fry for 2-3 minutes, or until the shallots and onions start to soften and turn golden.

Add this mixture and all the remaining ingredients to a large saucepan. Stir together thoroughly and cook on a medium heat for 15-20 minutes, or until the pumpkin is tender and the oil starts to separate.

Season to taste and finish with a handful of coriander leaves, if using, then serve.

SERVES: 4 PREP TIME: 15 COOKING TIME: 25 SPICE: 2/5

GAYANI'S STIR FRIED OKRA

1 tbsp coconut oil
1 tsp mustard seeds
½ tsp cumin seeds
1 sprig curry leaves
2 cloves of garlic, finely chopped
2½ cm piece rampe
(pandan leaf)
1 red onion, roughly chopped
¼ tsp turmeric powder
1½ tsp salt
300g okra
2 tsp Maldive fish flakes
1 level tsp dried chilli flakes
10 cherry tomatoes, halved

To prepare the okra, wash it, then snap off the tips where they break naturally (as you would with asparagus stalks). Chop into roughly 2½ cm pieces.

Place a large wok or frying pan on a medium heat and add the coconut oil. Once sizzling, add the mustard and cumin seeds. As soon as they start to spit, add the curry leaves, garlic, rampe, onion, turmeric and salt and stir with a wooden spoon.

Cook until browned slightly, then add the okra and stir again. Cook for 3 minutes then add the fish flakes, chilli flakes and tomatoes.

Continue cooking for another couple of minutes, letting the okra brown slightly, then remove from the heat and leave to cool.

Season to taste and serve.

SERVES: 4 PREP TIME: 15 COOKING TIME: 10 SPICE: 2/5

USEFUL FACT: Okra is extremely delicate and can become really slimy when overcooked so I watch the pan carefully when making this recipe.

BREADED PUMPKIN CUTLETS

400g pumpkin,
(peeled and cut into
2½ cm chunks)
1 tsp black mustard seeds
2 tsp cumin seeds
4 tbsp coconut oil
4 cloves of garlic, grated
1 red onion, finely chopped
5 shallots, finely chopped
3 fresh green chillies, chopped
2 tsp salt
1 tsp black pepper
½ tsp roasted curry powder
3 eggs, whisked
half a loaf of bread,
(made into breadcrumbs)
500ml vegetable oil
juice of ½ a lime
lime wedges, to serve

Boil the pumpkin in salted water for 10-15 minutes, or until soft. Remove with a slotted spoon and roughly mash.

Place a frying pan on a medium heat and dry roast the mustard and cumin seeds. When the mustard seeds begin to jump around in the pan and the cumin seeds turn golden immediately remove from the heat. Add to the mashed pumpkin and mix together, making sure the spices are evenly distributed.

Put the frying pan back on a medium heat and add a few tablespoons of coconut oil. Once sizzling, add the garlic, red onions, shallots, green chillies, remaining salt, pepper and curry powder. Fry for 3-4 minutes, or until the onions start to soften and turn golden brown. Remove from the heat then add to the mashed pumpkin, again mixing together thoroughly.

Roll the mixture into golf ball-sized pieces and repeat until you have used it all up. Dip the balls into the whisked egg, then the breadcrumbs. Repeat this process until all the balls are breaded.

Add the vegetable oil to a wok and place on a medium to high heat. Once sizzling, fry the pumpkin balls, a few at a time, until they are golden brown. Remove with a slotted spoon and leave to drain on kitchen towel. Serve with wedges of lime.

SERVES: 4 PREP TIME: 20 COOKING TIME: 25 SPICE: 2/5

RANJI'S CASHEW NUT CURRY

250g raw cashew nuts
2 tbsp coconut oil
½ tsp dill seeds
1 tsp mustard seeds
2 tsp cumin seeds
6 cloves of garlic, grated
3 fresh green chillies, chopped
1 red onion, roughly chopped
3 sprigs fresh curry leaves
250g fresh green peas
7½ cm piece rampe
(pandan leaf)
2 tsp roasted curry powder
5cm piece (½ stick) cinnamon
½ tsp curry power
½ tsp turmeric powder
1½ x 400ml tins of coconut milk
1 tsp salt
1 tsp black pepper
a handful of fresh coriander
(optional)

Boil the kettle. Place the cashews in a bowl and add enough boiling water to cover them. Cover with a lid or clean tea towel and leave to soak for around 30 minutes, then drain thoroughly.

Place a large high-sided frying pan on a medium heat and add the coconut oil. Once sizzling, add the dill, mustard and cumin seeds. As soon as the mustard seeds start to jump around, add the garlic, chillies, onion and curry leaves.

Fry for 2-3 minutes, or until the onions start to soften and turn golden.

Add this mixture and all the remaining ingredients to a large saucepan, cover and cook on a medium heat for 10 minutes, or until the oil starts to separate. Remove the lid and cook for a further 3 minutes.

Season to taste and finish with a handful of coriander leaves, if using, then serve.

SERVES: 4 PREP TIME: 35 COOKING TIME: 15 SPICE: 2/5

NIKKI'S CUCUMBER CURRY

1 large cucumber
1 x 400ml tin of coconut milk
3 fresh green chillies, chopped
4 cloves of garlic, grated
1 red onion, roughly chopped
5 shallots, roughly chopped
2 tsp curry powder
½ tsp turmeric powder
1 tsp roasted fenugreek seeds (crushed)
3 tbsp coconut oil
1 tsp black mustard seeds
2 sprigs fresh curry leaves
½ tsp salt
½ tsp black pepper
a handful of fresh coriander (optional)

To prepare the cucumber, peel it, then cut it in half lengthways. Push a teaspoon along the centre to remove the seeds and fibrous flesh. Discard these. Place each cucumber half cut side down on a chopping board and cut diagonally into roughly 1cm strips.

Set aside half of the coconut milk (200ml) and then add all the remaining ingredients (except the coconut oil, mustard seeds, curry leaves, seasoning and coriander) to a mixing bowl and combine thoroughly by hand.

Place a wok on a medium heat and add the coconut oil. Once sizzling add the mustard seeds and curry leaves. Fry for a minute until they spit and start to jump around in the pan.

Add the contents of the mixing bowl to the pan and stir briefly, then cover. Cook for 7-8 minutes, then add the remaining coconut milk. Bring to the boil and once the oil starts to separate, remove from the heat.

Season to taste and finish with a handful of coriander leaves, if using, then serve.

SERVES: 4 PREP TIME: 15 COOKING TIME: 10 SPICE: 2/5

WEST COAST CURRIED OKRA

400g okra
2 tbsp coconut oil
½ tsp black mustard seeds
2 sprigs fresh curry leaves
4 shallots, roughly chopped
2 fresh green chillies, chopped
½ red onion, roughly chopped
¼ tsp turmeric powder
¼ tsp curry powder
¼ level tsp chilli powder
7½ cm piece rampe
(pandan leaf)
1 stick cinnamon
1 x 400ml tin of coconut milk
½ tsp salt
1 tsp black pepper

To prepare the okra, wash it, then snap off the tips where they break naturally (as you would with asparagus stalks). Chop into roughly 2½ cm pieces.

Add the coconut oil to a high-sided frying pan on a medium heat. Once sizzling, add the mustard seeds and curry leaves. Once the mustard seeds start to spit, add the shallots, green chillies and red onion and fry until the onion starts to soften and turn golden. Add all the remaining ingredients and mix together thoroughly. Simmer for 10-12 minutes or until the oil starts to separate, stirring occasionally.

Season to taste and serve

SERVES: 4 PREP TIME: 10 COOKING TIME: 15 SPICE: 2/5

USEFUL FACT: Okra is a good source of vitamins A and C, as well as B complex vitamins, iron and calcium. It is low in calories, a good source of dietary fibre, and fat-free.

Motobike Diaries

MISSIONS ON THE MOTORBIKE

I'm going to be honest: the main roads in Sri Lanka are not the safest, due to the gung-ho style of some drivers. To navigate the roads successfully, you need a good horn, good brakes and, perhaps most importantly, good luck.

It follows that cruising around Sri Lanka on a motorbike can be dangerous, but I have been doing it for about 10 years now, so I know what to expect. You have to be fully alert at all times, as you will be battling with crowds of pedestrians, extremely erratic bus drivers, and the occasional suicidal dog…

After the tsunami, a mate of mine, Scotty, and I bought the family I have been staying with for the last 10 years a new Bajaj 125 motorbike from India so they could take my Sri Lankan little brother to school and generally get around. (They did have a bike but it was consumed by silt and seawater.) Every time I visit, the bike is mine for the taking and it has become my main travelling companion. I chuck my camera and a few essentials in my backpack and head off in search of new recipes and adventures. Being on a bike makes me feel totally free. My journeys are never really planned; there are no obligations.

Some of my best experiences on the island have come from my many bike trips. I might be invited to locals' houses for cups of sweet Sri Lankan tea, lunch or dinner. Sometimes I might end up staying with these hospitable and welcoming families for a few days or even weeks, cooking, gathering recipes and generally hanging out. When it's just me, the beloved Bajaj and the open road, then the possibilities are endless.

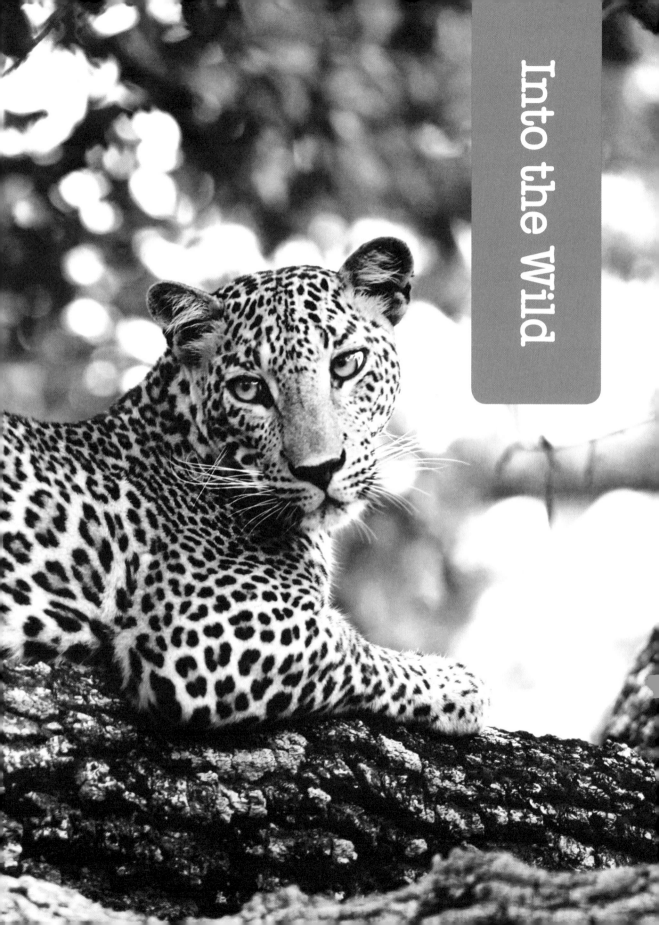

Into the wild

A LAND STALKED BY ONE OF NATURES MOST FEARED PREDATORS

Sri Lanka is highly ranked amongst the world's hot spots for biodiversity and has an incredible wealth of wildlife that belies its size. As a highly religious, predominantly Buddhist, culture, Sri Lankans have huge respect for animals and consider them to be sacred. Most of the island's wildlife is endemic to the country, so a high level of conservation needs to be maintained to ensure that its rich natural heritage is preserved.

The country has a large number of national parks, sanctuaries, and wetlands to accommodate its varied wildlife. Yala National Park, situated in the south-east region of the country, is definitely my favourite of the many places I have visited. It is a must see when visiting Sri Lanka, allowing you to encounter many species of birds, monkeys, crocodiles, lizards and much more.

Sri Lanka is stalked by one of nature's most feared predators: the leopard. It is the only leopard population in the world to have evolved as the top predator within its own eco-system. In India, leopards have to compete with tigers, and in Africa with lions, but on this little island, they can rest easy.

Home to 91 species of mammals, and with the surrounding oceans filled with blue whales, sperm whales, dolphins, and many sea turtles, the island is a dream for nature enthusiasts.

A macaque monkey posing for the camera on the East Coast.

TRACKING LEOPARDS IS NO EASY TASK

I first visited Yala in 2004, just days before the tragic tsunami that devastated the island. Although some animals were caught up in the wave, the majority had sensed the imminent threat and headed to higher ground long before the waves struck. On my next visit to the park in 2010, I was overwhelmed by the variation of species I encountered. Even though Sri Lanka has the highest density of leopards in the world, actually spotting them can be hit or miss. But on this day, I was in luck, and managed three sightings – I put this down to my guide, Diness, and his prayers at the temple the previous night.

Deep in thought.

Side Dishes

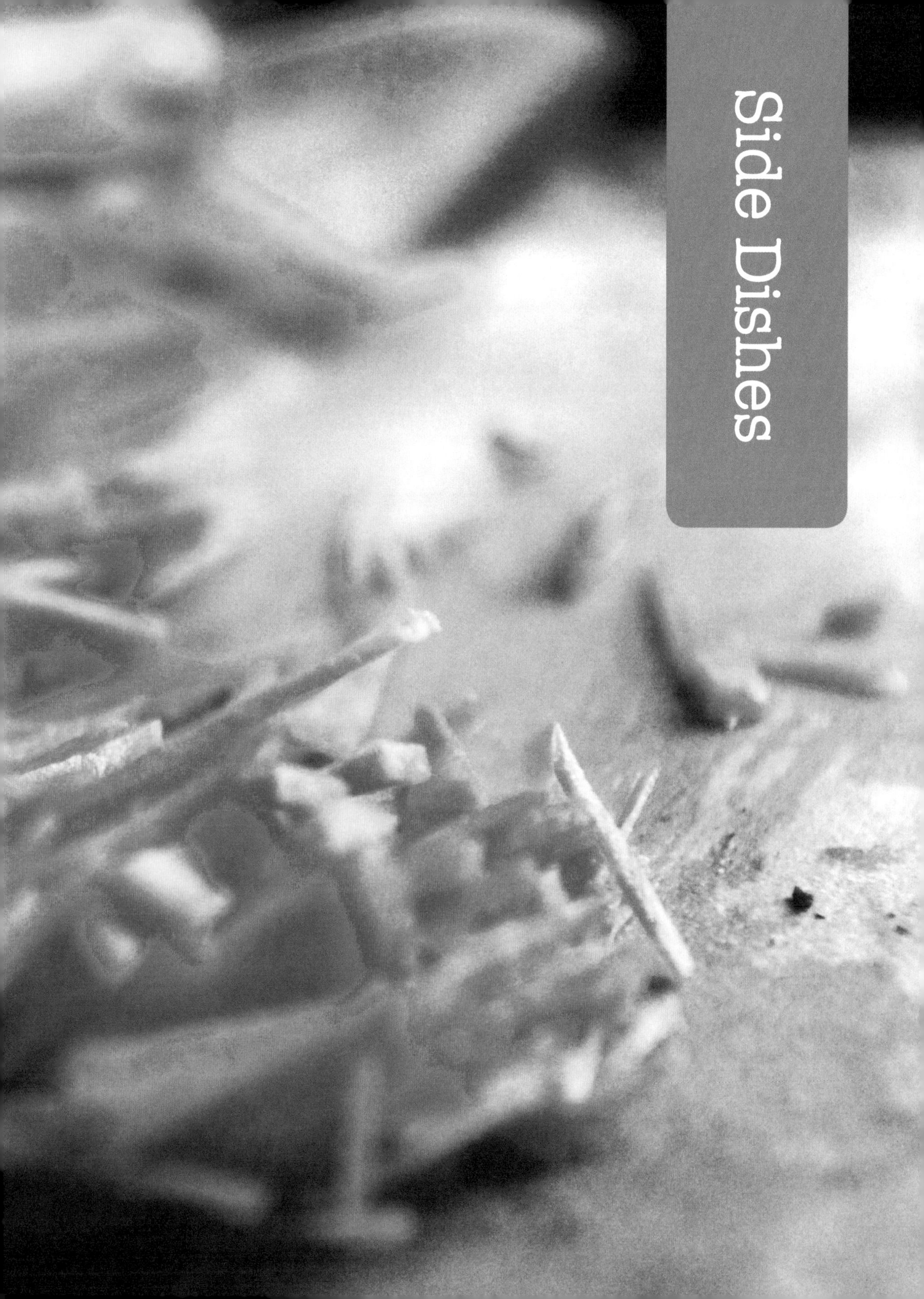

SEENI SAMBOL WITH SMALL DRIED FISH

100g small dried fish
2 tbsp coconut oil
3 cloves of garlic, grated
4 fresh green chillies, chopped
2½ cm piece ginger
2 red onions, roughly chopped
4 fresh tomatoes, diced
1 sprig fresh curry leaves
1 tsp curry powder
½ tsp black pepper
¼ tsp roasted fenugreek seeds (crushed)
¼ tsp turmeric powder
1 level tbsp dried chilli flakes
1 tbsp brown sugar
1½ tsp salt

Wash the dried fish in hot water then remove the heads and split down the centre by hand.

Place a small cooking pot on a medium heat and add the coconut oil. Once sizzling, add the fish. Fry, allowing them to take on a little colour, for around 2-3 minutes, stirring occasionally. Add the remaining ingredients then reduce the heat to low, cover and simmer for 30 minutes, stirring every so often.

Remove from the heat and allow to cool slightly then season to taste and serve.

SERVES: 4 PREP TIME: 15 COOKING TIME: 35 SPICE: 5/5

USEFUL FACT: Seeni sambol is a delicious caramelised onion relish. It is used both as a condiment and as a side dish. The traditional accompaniment to this is a coconut flat bread called Pol Roti, but it can also be served with any store bought bread of your choice, for a light lunch or snack or with an array of curries for a more substantial meal.

RANJI'S DHAL CURRY

100g red split lentils
1 bulb of garlic, grated
1 red onion, roughly chopped
2 tsp black mustard seeds
2 tsp cumin seeds
6 sprigs fresh curry leaves
2 fresh green chillies, chopped
¼ tsp turmeric powder
2 tsp ground coriander
1½ level tsp chilli powder
1 tsp salt
1 x 400ml tin of coconut milk
6 tbsp coconut oil

Ideally, you should soak the lentils in cold water for 2-3 hours to soften them up.

Set aside half the garlic, red onion, mustard and cumin seeds, and 3 sprigs of curry leaves.

Place the rest of the ingredients (except the coconut oil) into a medium sized saucepan. Mix together thoroughly by hand and cook on a medium heat for 10 minutes with a lid.

In another frying pan add the coconut oil and place on a medium heat. Once sizzling, add the reserved mustard seeds. As soon as they start to spit, add in the reserved cumin, garlic, red onion and curry leaves. Continue to fry and let the flavours infuse for a couple of minutes.

Pour this spiced oil (called tempered in Sri Lanka) on top of your finished dhal and swirl it in with a spoon. Season to taste and serve.

SERVES: 4 PREP TIME: 35 COOKING TIME: 25 SPICE: 3/5

GAYANI'S MINT SAMBOL

200g freshly ground coconut
2 handfuls of fresh mint leaves
(finely chopped)
1 clove of garlic, finely chopped
1 green chilli, roughly chopped
4 shallots, finely chopped
1 sprig curry leaves
¼ tsp brown sugar
½ tsp salt
¼ tsp black pepper

Mix the freshly grated coconut and chopped mint thoroughly, then add the remaining ingredients and again mix thoroughly.

If you would like your sambol a bit smoother then you could always mash it in a pestle and mortar.

Season to taste and serve.

SERVES: 4 PREP TIME: 10 COOKING TIME: 0 SPICE: 1/5

ZESTY CARROT SAMBOL

1 tbsp Maldive fish flakes
1 green chilli, roughly chopped
1 large carrot
(peeled and cut into matchsticks)
1 red onion, roughly chopped
¼ tsp salt
¼ tsp black pepper
juice of ½ a lime

Using a pestle and mortar, grind the dried fish flakes to a powder.

Add to a bowl, along with the chilli, carrot and red onion and mix together by hand.

Add the salt, pepper and lime juice and mix thoroughly again.

Season to taste and serve.

SERVES: 4 PREP TIME: 10 COOKING TIME: 0 SPICE: 1/5

DEVILLED CASHEWS

200ml vegetable oil
300g raw cashew nuts
4 sprigs fresh curry leaves
1 tsp chilli powder
½ tsp salt
½ tsp black pepper

Place a heavy bottomed frying pan on a medium to high heat and add the vegetable oil. Once sizzling hot and smoky, add the cashews and shallow fry, until golden brown. Make sure to move the nuts around with a slotted spoon so that they cook evenly.

Add the curry leaves for a few seconds then, using the slotted spoon, quickly remove both the nuts and curry leaves and leave to drain on kitchen towel.

Place the nuts and curry leaves in a bowl. Add the chilli, salt and pepper and toss together to combine.

These are best served with an ice-cold beer.

SERVES: 4 PREP TIME: 0 COOKING TIME: 5 SPICE: 4/5

RANJI'S SRI LANKAN SALAD

250g beetroot, peeled
4 tbsp coconut oil
100g mackerel fillets
1 large cucumber
(peeled and cut
into matchsticks)
3 carrots
(peeled and cut
into matchsticks)
6 fresh green chillies, chopped
3 red onions, roughly chopped
10 shallots, roughly chopped
½ tsp salt
½ tsp black pepper

Boil the peeled beets in a pan of salted water for 15 minutes, then drain and leave to cool.

Place a frying pan on a medium heat and add the vegetable oil. Once sizzling, add the mackerel. Cook on each side for around 2 minutes, or until the fish starts to flake apart. Remove from the heat and leave to cool.

Cut the cooked beetroot into slices around ½ cm thick and then into strips

Mix the mackerel and all the ingredients together, adding the beets last.

Season to taste and serve.

SERVES: 4 PREP TIME: 15 COOKING TIME: 0 SPICE: 3/5

TANGY MANGO CURRY

3 medium ripe mangoes, washed
1 tsp uncooked long grain rice
2 cardamom pods
¼ tsp black pepper
2 cloves
4 tbsp grated coconut
2 x 400ml tins of coconut milk
1 level tsp dried chilli flakes
2 tsp curry powder
2 tbsp vegetable oil
1 tsp mustard seeds
3 cloves of garlic, chopped
2½ cm piece of ginger
1 white bombay onion
3 fresh green chillies, chopped
1 sprig curry leaves
2½ cm piece of rampe
(pandan leaf)
½ stick cinnamon
2 tsp Maldive fish flakes
¼ tsp turmeric powder
3 tbsp sugar
1 tsp salt

Cut around the mango stones and roughly cut the flesh lengthways into strips. Don't throw away the stones as they can go into the curry too. (Once cooked you can suck the flesh from them – no waste in this kitchen...) Place the mango in a saucepan and cover with hot water. Set aside.

Place a frying pan on a low to medium heat and add the rice. Lightly toast until golden brown in colour. Add the cardamom seeds, pepper, cloves and grated coconut. Reduce the heat to low and cook for another couple of minutes. Remove from the heat altogether and add the coconut milk, chilli flakes and curry powder. Mix together well and set aside.

Next, place a wok on a medium heat and add the vegetable oil. Once sizzling, add the mustard seeds, garlic, ginger, onion and all the remaining ingredients (except the spiced coconut milk mixture).

Drain the water from the mangoes and add to the wok. Cover and simmer for 15 minutes, or until the oil starts to separate. Then add the spiced coconut milk mixture and bring to the boil.

Season to taste and serve.

SERVES: 4 PREP TIME: 15 COOKING TIME: 20 SPICE: 3/5

EAST COAST MANGO CHUTNEY

400g mangoes
(washed and cut
into 1cm cubes)
5 tsp salt
500ml white vinegar
10 shallots, finely chopped
4 cloves of garlic, crushed
2½ cm piece of ginger, grated
400g granulated sugar
1 tsp mustard powder
1 level tsp chilli powder

Place the cubed mango in a high-sided bowl and cover with salt. Mix together to ensure all the mango pieces are evenly coated. Cover the bowl with a tea towel and leave overnight. The next morning, drain any juice from the bowl and rinse the mango briefly with water.

Place a large saucepan on a low heat and add the vinegar, shallots, garlic, ginger, sugar and spices. Cook for around 6 minutes, or until all the sugar has dissolved and the shallots are golden brown. Turn up the heat and bring to the boil, then add the mango, reduce the heat back to low and simmer for 25 minutes. The mixture should become thick and sticky.

Leave to cool, then decant the chutney into sterilised jars, making sure there aren't any air pockets, and seal.

Your chutney is pretty much ready to go but it will get better over time so try not to use it all at once.

SERVES: 4 PREP TIME: 15 COOKING TIME: 35 SPICE: 1/5

DEEP FRIED SPRATS

250ml vegetable oil
200g sprats

These are super easy, super crunchy, lip-lickingly salty and great served with an ice-cold beer. I like to think of them as Sri Lanka's answer to a pork scratching.

Add the vegetable oil to a high-sided pan and place on a high heat. While it is heating up, you can remove the heads from the sprats if you wish, though I leave them on as they have a lot of flavour.

When the oil is sizzling hot, add the sprats and deep fry until golden brown. Remove using a slotted spoon and drain on some kitchen towel before serving.

SERVES: 4 PREP TIME: 5 COOKING TIME: 5 SPICE: 0/5

GAYANI'S LOTUS ROOT STIR FRY

1 litre water
500g fresh/tinned lotus root
3 tbsp coconut oil
¼ tsp black mustard seeds
½ tsp cumin seeds
1 clove of garlic, roughly chopped
1 sprig fresh curry leaves
2½ cm piece of (pandan leaf)
1 red onion, roughly chopped
2 fresh red chillies, finely chopped
1 tsp turmeric
1 piece of goraka
(soaked in hot water
for 20 minutes)
1 tsp roasted curry powder
1 tsp Maldive fish flakes
1 tsp salt
½ tsp black pepper

Place a large saucepan on a high heat and add the water and lotus root. Boil for around 25-30 minutes, or until the lotus root is still slightly al dente.

Remove from the heat, drain and leave to cool then peel and slice into 1cm discs.

Place a large high-sided frying pan or wok on a medium to high heat and add the coconut oil. Once sizzling, add the mustard seeds, cumin seeds, garlic, curry leaves and rampe. Fry for 30 seconds and then add the discs of lotus root. Fry for a couple of minutes, then add the onion, chilli, turmeric and goraka. Add the remaining ingredients, mix together well and continue frying until the lotus root is nicely browned.

Remove from the heat. Season to taste and serve.

SERVES: 4 PREP TIME: 25 COOKING TIME: 40 SPICE: 3/5

FIERY TOMATO SAMBOL

2 red onions, finely chopped
3 fresh green chillies, chopped
2 fresh red chillies, chopped
4 fresh tomatoes, diced
¼ tsp salt
½ tsp black pepper
juice of 1 lime

Place all the chopped and diced ingredients in a bowl then add the salt, pepper and lime juice. Mix together thoroughly by hand.

Season to taste and serve.

SERVES: 4 PREP TIME: 10 COOKING TIME: 0 SPICE: 4/5

COCONUT CHILLI SAMBOL

1 red onion, finely chopped
2 dried red chillies
1½ tsp chilli powder
½ level tsp chilli flakes
½ tsp salt
20g Maldive fish flakes
200g freshly grated coconut
juice of ½ a lime

Add all the ingredients except the coconut and lime juice to a pestle and mortar or blender. Mash or blend to a paste, making sure there are still a few coarse bits.

Add this mixture to a bowl along with the freshly ground coconut and mix together thoroughly by hand, ensuring the coconut is evenly coated with the red of the chilli mix.

Mix in the lime juice, season to taste and serve.

SERVES: 4 PREP TIME: 10 COOKING TIME: 0 SPICE: 5/5

EASY SRI LANKAN OMELETTE

4 eggs, whisked
½ tomato, diced
½ white onion, finely chopped
1 fresh green chilli,
finely chopped
2 cloves of garlic, crushed
1 sprig fresh curry leaves
½ leek, finely chopped
¼ tsp chilli flakes
2 tbsp water
¼ tsp salt
¼ tsp black pepper
1 tbsp coconut oil

Add the eggs and all the other ingredients (except the coconut oil) to a bowl and mix together.

Place a large frying pan, for which you have a lid, on a medium heat and add the coconut oil. Once sizzling, pour in the egg mixture, ensuring the base of the pan is covered. Put a lid on the frying pan and cook the omelette for 2-3 minutes.

The omelette should now be solid enough to toss but, if in doubt, place a plate on top of the pan, then flip it over, return the pan to the heat and slide the omelette back into the pan. Cook for a couple more minutes then season to taste and serve.

SERVES: 4 PREP TIME: 10 COOKING TIME: 10 SPICE: 2/5

SOUTHERN LIME PICKLE

25 limes
150g salt
1½ tsp chilli flakes
1 tsp cumin seeds
1 tsp cardamom pods
50g sugar
3 tbsp white vinegar
2 cloves of garlic, crushed
2½ cm piece of ginger, crushed
1 sprig curry leaves

Put 10 limes in a bowl, cover with cold water and leave to soak overnight. Drain the next morning. Place each lime on its base then, using a sharp knife, make a crossed cut halfway into each one.

Take a large high-sided bowl and add the soaked limes, again sitting each one on its base. Sprinkle with the salt, rubbing it in, then cover the bowl with a tea towel and leave overnight. The next morning, drain any juice from the bowl and rinse the limes with water.

Place a small frying pan on a low heat and roast the chilli flakes, cumin seeds and cardamom pods for 2 minutes. Grind into a coarse powder using a pestle and mortar. Set aside.

Juice the remaining 15 limes.

Place a large saucepan on a medium heat and add the lime juice together with the sugar, vinegar, garlic, ginger, curry leaves and roasted spices. Simmer for around 5 minutes and stir until the sugar has dissolved, then take off the heat and leave to cool. While you're waiting, chop the salted limes into small chunks and add these to the mixture, mixing together thoroughly.

Decant the lime pickle into sterilised jars, making sure there aren't any air pockets, then seal. Leave the jars on a south facing window sill for 5 days, ensuring they get plenty of sunlight and rotating on a daily basis (this helps them to slowly continue to cook in the jar, giving them more depth of flavour).

Place in the pantry and your pickle should be ready to eat in 4-5 weeks.

SERVES: 0 PREP TIME: 15 COOKING TIME: 20 SPICE: 4/5

Sri Lanka's Soul

CRICKET – THE SOUL OF SRI LANKA

Cricket is the most popular sport and pastime in Sri Lanka, without a shadow of a doubt. No matter where you are in the country, you can always find a game to get involved in. Whether you're playing with the locals on the beaches, or with the kids in the jungle, everyone is welcoming and it's always a lot of fun.

Cricket is played at all levels in Sri Lanka, from recreational games through to the semi professional and highly competitive professional games (which are watched almost religiously by the majority of the population). Having been to many live international matches in Sri Lanka, I can honestly say that they are a far cry from the somewhat dull and long-winded matches I've seen in the UK. The atmosphere is awesome, with many drummers, dancers and locals having the time of their lives, while the nation's heroes battle it out against their opponents.

The game was brought to the island during the 17th century with the British colonization and the national team now rank highly amongst the world's best (this transformation came about in the mid 90s). In 1996, the Sri Lankan team won the Cricket World Cup, defeating Australia in the final and they are still a team to be reckoned with.

An inter-village match, jungleside.

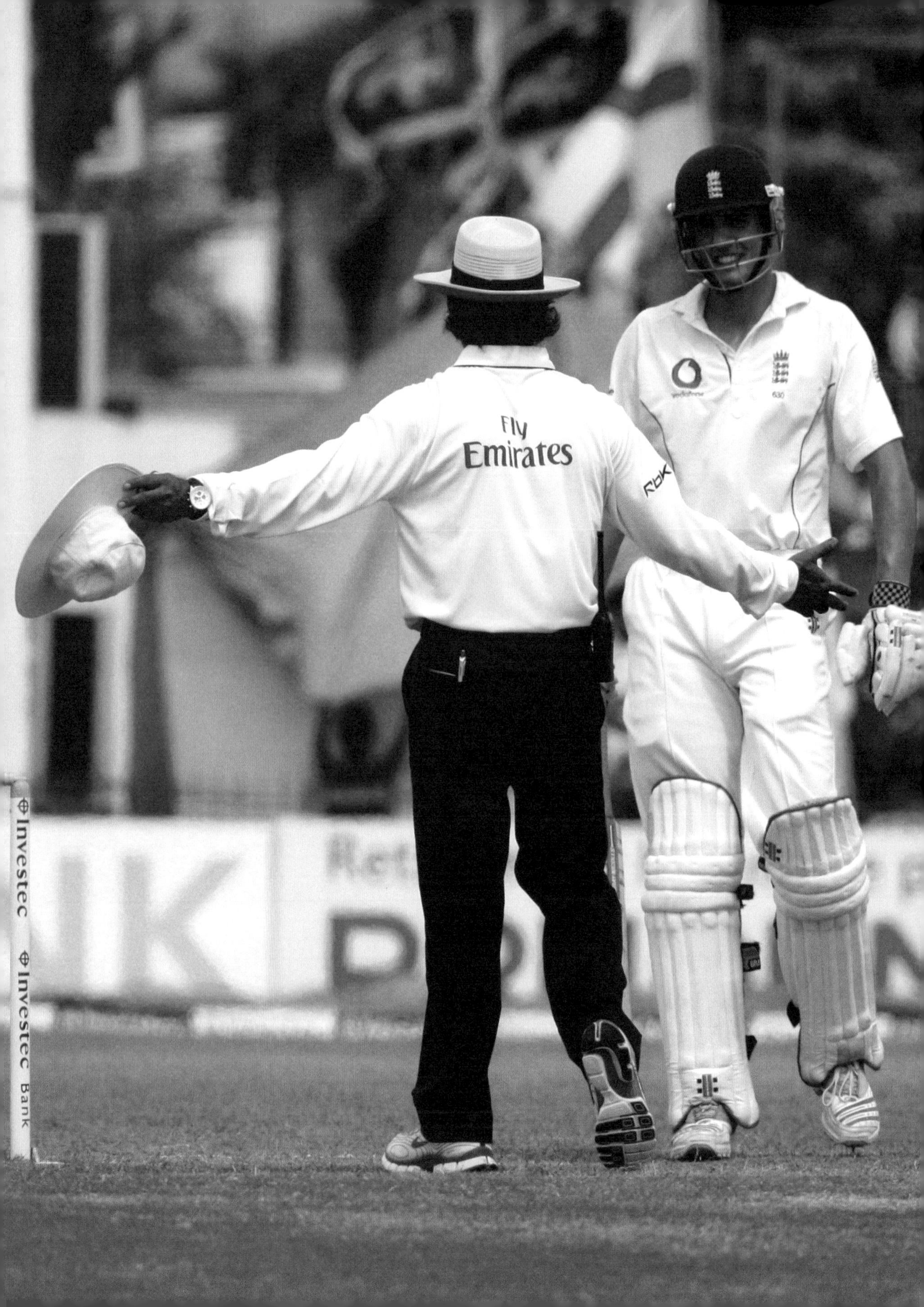
Fly
Emirates
Investec
Investec Bank

Lasith Malinga in action during a test against England back in 2007.

The Butchers

DEVILLED BEEF STIR FRY

400g beef fillet
4 tbsp of coconut oil
1 bulb of garlic,
roughly chopped
2 fresh green chillies
(roughly chopped)
4 red onions, roughly chopped
8 green capsicums
(or green peppers),
roughly chopped
1 leek, roughly chopped
4 fresh tomatoes, diced
½ tsp salt
1 tsp pepper
2 level tsp chilli powder
2 tbsp tomato sauce
2 tbsp oyster sauce
2 tsp soya bean sauce
a handful of fresh coriander
(optional)

FOR THE MARINADE:
juice of 1 lemon
1 tsp soya bean sauce
½ tsp salt
½ tsp black pepper

Place the beef fillet in a bowl and add the lemon juice, soya bean sauce and salt and pepper. Mix together thoroughly by hand and leave to marinate for 15 minutes.

When the beef has marinated, add half the coconut oil to a wok or high-sided frying pan and place on a high heat until it is as hot as you dare. Add the beef and fry for a few minutes on either side or until medium rare. Remove the beef with a slotted spoon and allow to rest.

Place the pan back on a medium heat and add the remaining coconut oil. Once sizzling, add the garlic and fry for a minute, then add the chillies, onions, peppers and leek. Cook for 5 minutes, add the tomatoes, salt, pepper, chilli powder, tomato sauce and oyster sauce.

Continue cooking on a medium heat for another 3 minutes, then slice the rested beef into 1cm strips and mix into the stir-fried vegetables.

Season to taste and finish with a handful of coriander leaves, if using, then serve.

SERVES: 4 PREP TIME: 20 COOKING TIME: 15 SPICE: 4/5

USEFUL FACT: This one definitely packs a punch so if you don't like things too hot then be sure to leave out a few chillies.

RANJI'S CHICKEN CURRY

500g chicken thighs, skin-on
3 tbsp coconut oil
5 cloves of garlic, grated
5 green chillies, roughly chopped
2 red onions, roughly chopped
3 sprigs of fresh curry leaves
4 tsp roasted curry powder
2 level tsp chilli powder
1 cinnamon stick
½ tsp salt
500ml chicken stock
125ml coconut milk
a handful of fresh coriander
(optional)

Take a wok or large frying pan, place on a high heat and add the coconut oil. Once sizzling, add the chicken and fry, skin side down, until the skin turns crisp and dark golden brown.

Add all the remaining ingredients (except the coconut milk and coriander) to a sauce pan and stir to combine. Cover and simmer on a medium to high heat for 15-20 minutes, or until the oil starts to separate, stirring occasionally.

Turn off the heat and leave to cool slightly then add the coconut milk and cook for 5 minutes on a low heat or until the chicken is cooked through. Season to taste and finish with a handful of coriander leaves, if using, then serve.

SERVES: 4 PREP TIME: 15 COOKING TIME: 30 SPICE: 4/5

DEVILLED PORK STIR FRY

400g pork fillet
(cut into 2½ cm pieces)
500ml vegetable oil
1 bulb of garlic, finely chopped
2 green chillies, finely chopped
4 red onions, roughly chopped
8 green capsicums
(or green peppers) chopped
1 leek, roughly chopped
4 fresh tomatoes, quartered
2 level tsp chilli powder
½ tsp salt
1 tsp pepper
2 tbsp tomato puree
2 tbsp oyster sauce

FOR THE MARINADE:
juice of 1 lemon
1 tsp soya bean sauce
½ tsp salt
½ tsp black pepper

Add the pork, lemon juice, soya bean sauce, and salt and pepper to a bowl. Mix together thoroughly and leave to marinate for 5 minutes.

Add the vegetable oil to a wok or high-sided frying pan and place on a high heat until very hot. Add the pork, a few pieces at a time, and cook until golden brown. Set aside.

Place a large frying pan on a medium heat and add a dash of vegetable oil. Once sizzling, add the garlic, fry for a minute, and then add the chillies, onions, capsicums and leek. Cook for 5 minutes, then add the tomatoes, chilli powder, salt, pepper, tomato puree and oyster sauce.

Continue cooking for 3 minutes, then remove from the heat and toss in your deep fried pork.

Season to taste and finish with a handful of coriander leaves, if using, then serve.

SERVES: 4 PREP TIME: 15 COOKING TIME: 20 SPICE: 4/5

GAYANI'S LAMB CURRY

400g lamb chops
1 tsp salt
½ tsp black pepper
2 tsp roasted curry powder
¼ tsp chilli powder
3 tbsp coconut oil
½ tsp cumin seeds
1 sprig of curry leaves
2½ cm piece of rampe
(pandan leaf)
4 cloves of garlic, crushed
5cm piece of ginger, crushed
½ a red onion, roughly chopped
1 fresh green chilli, chopped
350ml water
3 pieces of goraka
(soaked in hot water
for 20 minutes)
125ml coconut milk
1 medium sized potato, diced
½ tsp turmeric powder
2½ cm piece of cinnamon

Add the lamb chops, salt, pepper, half the roasted curry powder and half the chilli powder, to a large bowl. Mix together thoroughly by hand, making sure that each piece of lamb is evenly coated. Leave to marinate for around 10-15 minutes.

Add the garlic and ginger to a pestle and mortar and mash into a paste.

Place a wok or high-sided frying pan on a medium to high heat and add the coconut oil. Once sizzling, add the cumin seeds, curry leaves and rampe. Allow the flavours to infuse for 30 seconds and then add the marinated lamb. Fry for 3-4 minutes, or until the lamb starts to brown nicely. Add the garlic, ginger, onions and chilli to the pan and fry for 3 minutes, then add the water, goraka, potato, turmeric, cinnamon and remaining curry and chilli powder.

Reduce the heat to low then cover and simmer for an hour and a quarter, stirring occasionally. Remove from the heat, stir in your coconut milk and allow the curry to cool slightly. Season to taste and serve.

SERVES: 4 PREP TIME: 25 COOKING TIME: 120 SPICE: 2/5

HIGHLAND PORK CURRY

4 tbsp coconut oil
8 dried red chillies, chopped
4 red onions, finely chopped
8 garlic cloves, finely chopped
2½ cm piece of ginger
1 lemongrass stalk, bruised
3 sprigs of fresh curry leaves
juice of 1 lime
500g pork fillet
(cut into 2½ cm pieces)
1 tsp salt
2 tsp black pepper
2 green chillies, chopped
3 tsp roasted curry powder
1 litre water

Heat half the oil in a wok or high-sided frying pan, then add the dried chillies and fry until they turn dark red. Remove from the heat and place into a mortar with the onions, garlic, ginger, lemongrass, curry leaves and lime juice. Bash them with the pestle (or you could use a food processor) until you have a smooth, fine paste.

Place the pork in a bowl and smother with the paste, making sure they are all evenly coated. Season with salt and black pepper then leave to marinate for 30 minutes.

Place a wok on a medium to high heat, add the rest of the coconut oil and, once sizzling, add the pork. Brown off the meat, then add to a sauce pan along with the chillies, roasted curry powder and water.

Bring to a boil then reduce to a simmer, cover the pan and cook for about an hour and a half, or until the meat is completely tender and the oil starts to separate. Keep an eye on it and add a bit more water if it looks like it is drying out.

Season to taste and serve.

SERVES: 4 PREP TIME: 35 COOKING TIME: 95 SPICE: 3/5

DEVILLED CHICKEN STIR FRY

400g chicken legs and thighs
(cut into 2½ cm pieces)
500ml vegetable oil, plus 2 tbsp
1 bulb of garlic, roughly chopped
2 fresh green chillies, chopped
4 red onions, roughly chopped
8 green capsicums
(or green peppers), roughly chopped
1 leek, roughly chopped
4 fresh tomatoes, quartered
2 level tsp chilli powder
½ tsp salt
1 tsp pepper
2 tsp soya bean sauce
2 tbsp tomato sauce
2 tbsp oyster sauce
a handful of fresh coriander
(optional)

FOR THE MARINADE:
juice of 1 lemon
1 tsp soya bean sauce
½ tsp salt
½ tsp black pepper

Add the chicken, lemon juice, soya bean sauce and salt and pepper to a bowl. Mix together thoroughly and leave to marinate for 5 minutes.

Add the vegetable oil to a wok or high-sided frying pan and place on a high heat until very hot. Add the chicken, a few pieces at a time, and cook until golden brown. Set aside.

Place a large frying pan on a medium heat and add 2 tablespoons of vegetable oil. Once sizzling, add the garlic, fry for a minute, and then add the chillies, onions, capsicums and leek.

Cook for 5 minutes, then add the tomatoes, chilli powder, salt, pepper, tomato sauce and oyster sauce.

Continue cooking for 3 minutes, then remove from the heat and toss in your deep fried chicken. Season to taste and finish with a handful of coriander leaves, if using, then serve.

SERVES: 4 PREP TIME: 15 COOKING TIME: 25 SPICE: 4/5

USEFUL FACT: There are many devilled dishes in Sri Lanka but devilled chicken has to be my favourite, with its sweet and sour flavours tantalizing the tastebuds.

NIKKI'S BEEF CURRY

3½ tsp roasted curry powder
2½ tsp chilli powder
500g beef chuck steak, diced
3 tbsp vinegar
3 tbsp coconut oil
(plus an extra splash)
2 red onions, roughly chopped
6 cloves of garlic, grated
2 fresh green chillies, chopped
2 sprigs of fresh curry leaves
2 fresh tomatoes, diced
½ tsp cumin seeds
1 tsp salt
500ml of water
1 x 400ml tin of coconut milk
a handful of fresh coriander
(optional)

Place a small frying pan on a low heat and add the curry and chilli powder. Dry roast for around 2-3 minutes, stirring occasionally, then take off the heat.

Add the beef, vinegar and roasted spices to a bowl and mix together thoroughly by hand, making sure that each piece of meat is evenly coated.

Place a wok or large pan on a medium heat and add the coconut oil. Once sizzling, add the onions, garlic and chillies. Fry until the onions start to soften and turn golden brown then add the curry leaves. Push everything to one side of the wok and add a little more coconut oil. Once hot, add the diced beef and cook until nicely browned, then add in the tomatoes, cumin and salt and stir.

Add any marinade left over in the bowl used for seasoning the beef to 500ml of water. Mix together and add to the wok.

Turn to a low heat, cover and simmer for 75 minutes, then add the coconut milk. Bring to the boil, then remove from the heat. Season to taste and finish with a handful of coriander leaves, if using, then serve.

SERVES: 4 PREP TIME: 15 COOKING TIME: 90 SPICE: 4/5

GAYANI'S CHICKEN CURRY

500g chicken thighs, skin on
1 tsp salt
1 tsp black pepper
3 tbsp coconut oil
1 sprig of fresh curry leaves
4 cardamom pods
½ tsp cumin seeds
2½ cm piece of rampe
(pandan leaf)
½ tsp chilli powder
1 tbsp paprika
2 pieces goraka
(soaked in hot water
for 20 minutes)
500ml water
4 cloves of garlic, grated
5cm piece of ginger, grated
1 fresh green chilli, finely chopped
1 red onion, roughly chopped
7½ cm piece of cinnamon
4 cloves
2½ tsp roasted curry powder
½ tsp roasted fenugreek seeds
(crushed)
1 tbsp freshly roasted coconut
1 tsp turmeric powder

Season the chicken thighs.

Place a large frying pan on a high heat and add the coconut oil. Once sizzling, add the curry leaves, cardamom pods, cumin seeds and rampe.

Fry for 30 seconds, then add the chicken thighs, skin side down. Then add the chilli powder and paprika.

Once the chicken skin has crisped up nicely (around 5 minutes), turn the thighs over and add the goraka, water and all remaining ingredients.

Reduce the heat to low to medium and cover. Cook for 25-30 minutes or until the chicken is cooked through (pierce it to check if you are unsure).

Take off the heat and allow to cool slightly.

Season to taste and serve.

SERVES: 4 PREP TIME: 25 COOKING TIME: 35 SPICE: 3/5

GOAT CURRY

500g goat chump chops, bone in
1½ tsp salt
1 tsp pepper
3 tsp roasted curry powder
½ tsp chilli powder
6 cloves of garlic
5cm piece of ginger
4 tbsp coconut oil
1 tsp cumin seeds
1 sprig of fresh curry leaves
10cm piece rampe (pandan leaf)
1 red onion, roughly chopped
1 white onion, roughly chopped
2 green chillies, finely chopped
1 fresh red chilli, finely chopped
750ml water
150ml coconut milk
juice of ½ a lime
10cm piece of cinnamon

Place the goat chops, salt, pepper, half of the curry powder and half of the chilli powder in a large bowl and mix together thoroughly by hand, ensuring the meat is evenly coated. Leave to marinate for around half an hour.

Add the garlic and ginger to a pestle and mortar with around 2 tbsp of water and mash into a paste.

Place a wok or high-sided frying pan on a medium to high heat and add the coconut oil. Once sizzling, add the cumin seeds, curry leaves and rampe. Allow the flavours to infuse for 30 seconds and then add the marinated goat. Fry the goat for 2-3 minutes on each side or until it starts to brown nicely.

Add the garlic and ginger paste, onions and chillies to the pan and fry for 3 minutes, then add the water along with the cinnamon and remaining curry and chilli powder.

Reduce the heat to low to medium and simmer, stirring occasionally, for 40 minutes or until the meat is nice and tender. Take off the heat, stir in the coconut milk and allow to cool slightly before squeezing in the lime juice. Season to taste and serve

SERVES: 4 PREP TIME: 35 COOKING TIME: 40 SPICE: 3/5

THE ROLLING HIGHLANDS

The rolling hills of the Sri Lankan highlands are carpeted with some of the best tea plantations in the world. Oddly enough, the story of Ceylon tea actually started with coffee as the first British settlers initially saw the diverse climate and sloping hills as ideal for coffee plantations.

In the 19th century, the Sri Lankan highlands were decimated by disease which wiped out the coffee industry and, as the popularity of tea grew throughout the world, the story of Ceylon tea began in Nuwara Eliya, the heart of the Sri Lankan tea industry.

The hill country's tea plantations have been a great asset to the Sri Lankan economy for centuries, and the industry itself provides jobs for more than a million people. The majority of the workforce are women of Tamil origin and even today the pay rate remains astonishingly low. Campaigns are now in place in many tea plantation areas to transform estates into fair trade establishments, giving the workers a fair price for their hard work.

Having visited many plantations over the last 10 years, I have an enormous amount of respect for the tea workers. They pick and sort the tea come rain or shine, often in the most extreme temperatures and humidity and are required to pick at least 20kg per day – not an easy task.

Drying troughs at a factory in Nuwara Eliya, the
heart of Sri Lankan tea.

ENTRY RESTRICTED
AUTHORIZED
PERSONNEL ONLY

THE PROCESS

What makes Ceylon tea so special is the way the leaves are picked. Without a shadow of a doubt, hand picking produces the best tea in the world as it ensures that the leaves are not bruised or damaged in any way.

Once the tea leaves are picked, they are taken into one of the many factories where they are laid out in troughs and dried by enormous fans to remove any excess moisture. Once dry, the leaves are rolled, twisted and then crushed, which speeds up the fermentation process. The crushed leaves are then exposed to high temperatures and left to ferment. This process has to be monitored carefully as fermentation fluctuates depending on temperature and humidity, and the flavour of the leaves can be greatly altered if they are left for too long.

Once the process is complete, the tea has to be graded. This is done using a variety of different sized meshes, which sort the tea particles according to their shape and size. Any sub-standard tea that fails to comply with standards is rejected regardless of quantity and value. The tea is then inspected further and packed into paper sacks ready to be exported.

The highlands of this beautiful island really are spectacular, with the tea pickers canvased against the vibrant backdrop of the rolling green hills.

The climate is also a nice change from the sweltering heat of beach life and is known to the Sri Lankan's as 'little England', due to its cooler climate.

NETT : 55 0 0 GRADE : G S 1
TARE : 70 BAG NO 2 20
GROSS: 70 INV. NO :
55 70 253

LABOOKELLIE

TEA PRODUCE

Agalawatte Plantations Limited
MACKWOODS
Estd. 1841
Managing Agents
Mackwoods Plantations(Pvt)Limited

NETT : 55 0 0 GRADE G S 1
TARE : 7 0 BAG NO : 9 20
GROSS: INV. NO :
55 70 253

LABOOKELLIE

GROSS:	SS	INV. NO :	52
TARE :		BAG NO :	1
NETT : S S		GRADE : C S	

SRI LANKA

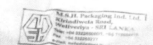

M.S.H. Packaging Ind. Ltd.
Kiriadiwela Road,
Weliweriya - SRI LANKA.

LABOOKELLIE

VINDI'S LIME JUICE

juice of 4 limes or lemons
300ml soda water
4 tbsp granulated sugar
3 cubes ice, crushed

To get the most from your limes, roll them one at a time across the kitchen counter. This loosens them up, making it easier to extract their juice.

Slice the limes in half and squeeze over a bowl – if using lemons, use your other hand to catch the pips. If necessary, get a fork and twist it into the remaining flesh of each half of lime or lemon, to extract any extra juice.

Add the juice, soda water, sugar and crushed ice to a blender and blitz. Have a taste –if it is still too bitter then add a little more sugar. If you find it too sweet, just add more lime juice. If you don't have any soda, water is just as good.

SERVES: 1 PREP TIME: 5

FRESH PINEAAPPLE JUICE

150g pineapple
200ml water
2 tbsp granulated sugar
4 cubes ice, crushed
juice of ¼ lime

Using a sharp knife, cut off the base and the top of the pineapple so that it sits flat on the chopping board. Remove the skin by cutting down the length of the pineapple, being careful not to remove too much flesh.

Remove the eyes of the pineapple by using a paring knife to cut a shallow trench that spirals around each eye.

Slice the pineapple into discs and remove the hard core, then cut into cubes.

Add the pineapple discs, water, sugar, crushed ice and lime juice to a blender and blitz until you have reached a smooth-ish consistency.

Serve immediately while still cold.

SERVES: 1 PREP TIME: 5

FRESH WATERMELON JUICE

300g watermelon
3 cubes of ice, crushed
granulated sugar, to taste

Slice the watermelon into wedges, then scoop the flesh into the blender and add the crushed ice and sugar.

You shouldn't need any additional liquid as watermelon contains a lot of water.

You might like to remove the seeds first, but I tend to leave them in as they aren't harmful, and blend the juice until the seeds are blended too.

SERVES: 1 PREP TIME: 5

PASSION FRUIT JUICE

5 passion fruits
300ml water
3 cubes of ice, crushed
2 tbsp granulated sugar
juice of ½ a lime

Cut the passion fruits in half, scoop out the insides and add to the blender.

Add the water, crushed ice, sugar and lime juice to the blender and blitz.

Serve while still cold.

SERVES: 1 PREP TIME: 5

PINEAPPLE LASSI

150g pineapple
3 cubes of ice, crushed
100g curd or natural yoghurt
2 tbsp sugar

Peel and chop the pineapple then add to a blender with the ice, yoghurt and sugar.

Blitz to a pulp.

Serve immediately while still cold.

SERVES: 1 PREP TIME: 5

LIME LASSI

juice of 2 limes
3 tbsp sugar
3 cubes of ice, crushed
100g curd or natural yoghurt

To get the most from your limes, roll them one at a time across the kitchen counter. This loosens them up, making it easier to extract their juice. Slice them in half and squeeze the juice out over a bowl.

Add the sugar to the lime juice, add the curd or yoghurt then blitz in a food processor and serve.

Out of all the lassis I've tried, this has to be my favourite – it is like a cheesecake in a glass (minus the buttery biscuit base, of course).

SERVES: 1 PREP TIME: 5

MANGO LASSI

250g mango
2 tbsp sugar
3 cubes of ice, crushed
100g curd (or natural yoghurt)

Using a flexible knife, cut down the centre of the mango around the stone and repeat on the other side. Score each half with a criss cross pattern, turn inside out and scoop out the cubes.

Add to a blender with the sugar and ice and blend to a pulp. Decant into a glass, setting aside 20ml, then pour in the curd or yoghurt. Finish off with the remaining pulp and serve immediately.

As with all juices and lassis, sugar is optional so if you don't like it too sweet, just leave it out.

SERVES: 1 PREP TIME: 5

BANANA LASSI

4 small or 2 large bananas
2 tbsp sugar
3 cubes of ice, crushed
100g curd or natural yoghurt

Peel and slice the bananas then add to a blender, along with the sugar and ice and yoghurt or curd. Blitz to a pulp and serve.

Perfect as a pre-surf drink: I have one every morning before heading out.

I like my banana lassi quite thick, but this is personal preference.

SERVES: 1 PREP TIME: 5

KOLA KANDA

Kola Kanda is a traditional Sri Lankan drink made up of a variety of green leaves and herbs, the main ingredient being gotu kola, a medicinal herb used all over the island. It is mixed together with coconut milk, rice and salt, and is often served with jaggery, a sweet treat that complements the flavours and caters for sweet tooths. I tend to drink it without the jaggery as I like the healthy green flavours. Kola Kanda is a nutritious and wholesome start to the day and, when I am on the island, I go down to the local harbour every morning at sunrise to get my dose. The positive impact that comes from drinking this traditional and natural drink is amazing. Research into the medicinal properties of Kola Kanda has shown that it is often used as a remedy for many ailments, and is especially used in Ayurvedic practices. It might sound too good to be true, but I've recommended it to everyone I've met and have never heard a complaint!

The Holy Mountain

A MISSION TO ADAM'S PEAK

Our journey began in Hikkaduwa at 7am. Banana leaf-wrapped Sri Lankan lunch packet in hand, we made our way to the train station. The three-hour train ride to the capital is stunning – the track pretty much runs alongside the coastline. The train was packed as usual, and although there was no chance of getting a seat, the doors remained open, so we took up our usual spot, perched on the edge of the open door and watched the picturesque coastal landscape rush by.

Once we arrived in the capital, we hung out in the station, chatting with a few locals who were keen to practice their English, before boarding another train to take us on the next leg – Columbo to Hatton. This journey was even more breathtaking than the last, and is ranked as one of the top 5 train rides in the world. It's not hard to see why; the views were outstanding as we gracefully moved through the rolling hills of the central highlands. Once

in Hatton, we began the final part of our journey to the small settlement of Dalhousie, which lies at the base of the peak.

Located in central Sri Lanka, Adam's Peak (or Sri Pada in Sinhalese) is a 2243m high mountain. It is deemed holy by many different religions and it holds a large footprint protected by a temple at the summit of the mountain. This is thought to be the place where Adam first set foot on the earth and many Buddhists believe that this footprint is of Buddha himself and where he took his first steps to enlightenment.

Climbing this holy mountain is no easy task, as there are 5,200 steps to the summit. These steps are very irregular in shape and size, and it takes between 2-4 hours to get to the top. I recently undertook this mission with some good friends, and although extremely hard work, it was sensational in every way.

A mid mountain pitstop
on route to Hatton.

5,200 STEPS TO THE TOP

We started the mammoth climb at 2:30am in pitch darkness. I thought it was going to be easy as I'd been surfing 2-3 times a day for the last 4 months, and my fitness levels were pretty good. After about 2 hours of climbing, it became apparent to me that this was not the case. As with climbing any mountain at high altitudes, the air gets thinner the higher you go, and I had to take a break to catch my breath. While sitting and taking a much-needed sip of water, I saw three elderly ladies and two young children powering up the mountain with a very determined look in their eyes. It was then that I realized that this mammoth task was all in the mind. If they could climb at that pace, so could I. We powered on through and reached the summit half an hour later. We'd started the climb in the early hours of the morning to get to the top for the sunrise. We were just in time and joined hundreds of others, tourists and locals alike, to see the first rays of light shoot out from the horizon.

There is a Buddhist temple at the summit, along with with many shrines catering for the different religions that visit this holy mountain. As the sun rose, the sound of drums and what sounded to me like some form of Sri Lankan bagpipe bellowed out. It was an amazingly spiritual experience; one I will never forget. The sunrise and views from each side of the peak were spectacular.

A rare sight, an empty carriage on the
way home from Adam's Peak.

Sweet Things

DELICIOUS MILK TOFFEE

500ml condensed milk
125g white sugar
10g unsalted butter

Take a saucepan and place on a low heat. Add the condensed milk and 100g of the sugar, stirring constantly.

In a separate pan, heat the remaining 25g of sugar together with half the butter until golden brown and caramelized. Make sure to stir constantly, as this is what gives this sweet treat its colour.

Add the caramel to the condensed milk mixture and simmer for 20-25 minutes, or until it is bubbling and becomes stiff in texture.

Rub a chopping board or ridgeless baking tray with the remaining butter. Spread the thick toffee mixture on to the buttered board and pat down with cling film until around 1½ cm thick. You should end up with a relatively smooth finish. Leave to cool for around 10 minutes then cut into bite size pieces.

SERVES: 4 PREP TIME: 10 COOKING TIME: 30

NARANG KAVUM

10g rice flour
250g sugar
120ml water
250g freshly grated coconut
¼ litre vegetable oil

FOR THE BATTER MIX:

100g plain flour
20g rice flour
½ tsp salt
a pinch of turmeric powder
50ml coconut milk

To make the batter mix, sift the flours into a mixing bowl and add the salt and turmeric. Then add the coconut milk and whisk until there are no lumps. Set aside.

Take a large frying pan and place on a low heat. Add the rice flour and roast for 4-5 minutes making sure that it doesn't burn. Set aside.

Add the sugar to another pan and put on a low to medium heat. Once it starts to caramelize slightly, add the water and mix together. Simmer for around 7-8 minutes or until it turns golden brown and starts to thicken.

Add the fresh coconut to the roasted rice flour and mix together.

Reduce the heat on the caramel pan to low then add the coconut and roasted rice flour. Cook for 7-8 minutes, stirring constantly.

Remove from the heat and transfer to a large bowl. When cool enough to handle, make the caramelized coconut into golf ball sized pieces.

Place a wok on a medium heat and add the vegetable oil. Once sizzling, dip your balls into the batter and deep fry, a few at a time, until golden brown.

Drain on newspaper or kitchen towel and serve.

SERVES: 4 PREP TIME: 15 COOKING TIME: 20

ALUWA

200g rice flour
150g white sugar
250ml water
a good pinch of salt

Sieve the rice flour into a bowl.

Place a large frying pan on a medium heat, add 180g of the rice flour and roast for around 3-4 minutes. Stir constantly to stop it from burning.

Place another pan on a low heat and add the sugar, water and salt. Simmer for 2-3 minutes only (you're not trying to caramelize the mixture). Set aside and leave to cool. Gradually add the roasted rice flour to the sugar and water mix, stirring constantly until it becomes stiff.

Take a chopping board and generously dust with the remaining rice flour. Place the mixture on to the board and flatten it by hand until it is around 1½ cm thick. It should be solid and relatively brittle. Use a sharp knife to cut it into squares.

SERVES: 4 PREP TIME: 5 COOKING TIME: 10

KOKIS

250g plain flour
50g rice flour
1 egg
400ml coconut milk
a pinch of salt
1 tsp turmeric powder
250ml vegetable oil

For this recipe you will need a special kokis mould.

Sift both types of flour into a large mixing bowl. Make a well in the centre and break the egg into the mix. Mix by hand for a minute and then gradually add the coconut milk, salt and turmeric, and whisk until smooth. Leave to sit for around 30 minutes.

Place a wok on a medium to high heat. Add the vegetable oil and heat until sizzling.

Heat up the mould itself for a few minutes in the oil.

Once the mould is heated, carefully dip into the batter mix, taking care not to submerge it completely. Remove from the batter and place into the hot oil. After around 30 seconds, the batter should separate from the mould (if it sticks ease it off by tapping the mould with a spoon).

Cook until golden brown and repeat the process until all the batter is used up.

SERVES: 4 PREP TIME: 35 COOKING TIME: 10

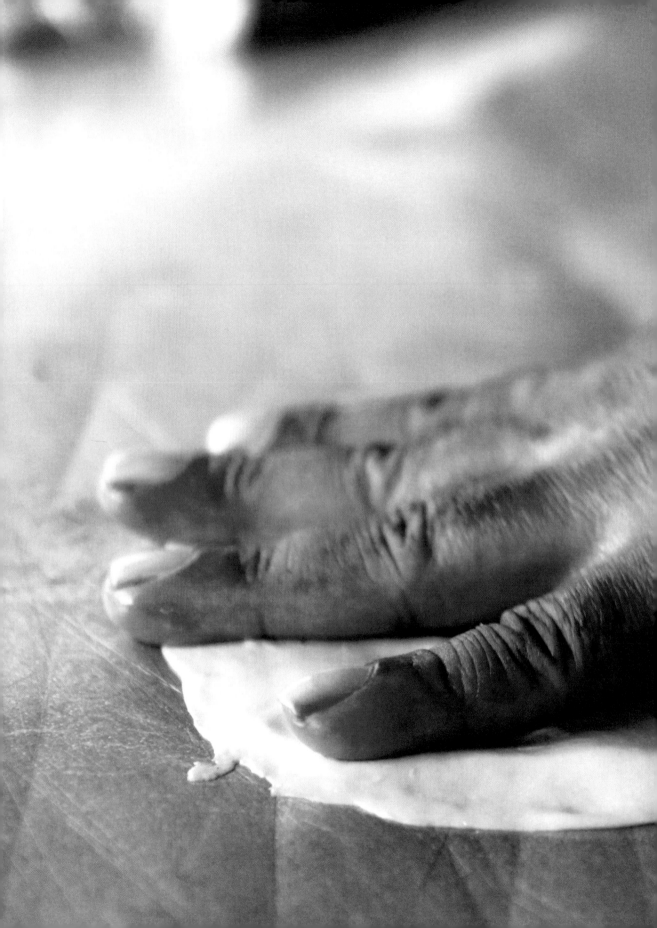

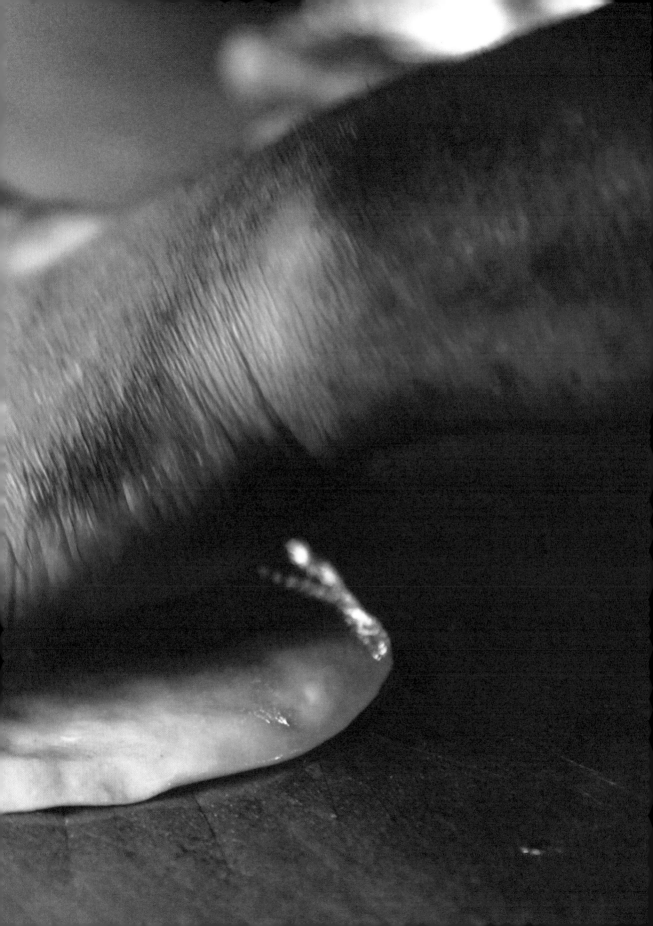

TRADITIONAL MILK RICE

450g basmati rice
500ml of water
2 x 400ml tins of coconut milk
1 tsp salt

Thoroughly wash the rice in a sieve under running water until it runs clear. This will remove the starch.

Place a saucepan on a high heat and add 500ml of water. Add the rice and boil for around 10 minutes until all the water has been absorbed. Now add the coconut milk, turn to a low heat and again simmer until it has all been absorbed. Remove the rice from the pan and allow to cool. Once cooled, place on a smooth surface. Flatten out using a banana leaf or cling film paper. Push into a firm round shape and cut into diamond shaped pieces.

Remove the rice from the pan and place on a smooth surface. Flatten out using a banana leaf or greaseproof paper. Push into a firm round shape and cut into diamond shaped pieces.

SERVES: 4 PREP TIME: 0 COOKING TIME: 25

USEFUL FACT: Instead of using a knife, the traditional Sri Lankan way of cutting milk rice is to wrap a piece of banana leaf around the handle of a spoon and use this. This stops the pieces splitting and falling apart.

DEEP FRIED KAVUM

50g white sugar
250ml water
25g rice flour
200g plain flour
a good pinch of salt
250ml vegetable oil

Place a small pan on a low, gentle heat, add half the sugar and cook for 3-4 minutes. Once slightly caramelized, add almost all of the water (leaving around 100ml) and simmer for another couple of minutes, then set aside.

Sift the rice flour, wheat flour, salt and the remaining sugar into a large bowl, and add the remaining water. Mix together by hand until it becomes a dough.

Gradually add in the caramel and water mixture, continuing to bring it together by hand. You want a batter with a similar consistency to a pancake mix. When it reaches this stage leave it to sit for 15 minutes.

Place a wok on a medium heat and add the vegetable oil. Once sizzling, take half a ladle full of your batter and gently pour into the centre of the wok. It will expand into a ball shape. Fry until golden brown – this should only take a few minutes. Repeat the process until you have used up all the batter mix. Leave the balls to drain on kitchen towel.

SERVES: 4 PREP TIME: 10 COOKING TIME: 15

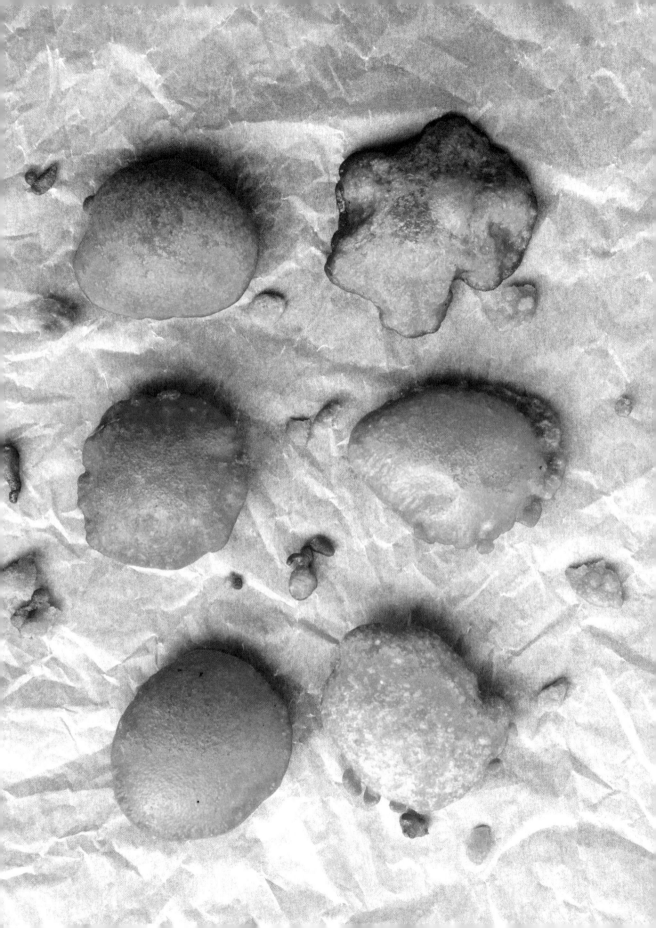

PANNI WALALU

100g undu flour
100ml coconut milk
half a large banana
250g rice flour
250g white sugar
120ml water
500ml coconut oil
a good pinch of salt

Add the undu flour, coconut milk and banana into the blender and blitz into a paste. Once blended, take out and place in a large mixing bowl. Gradually add the rice flour, a little at a time, mixing constantly by hand until a doughy consistency is achieved. Your mixture should be half way between a batter and a dough – not too thick, but not too thin. Cover with cling film and leave to sit for an hour and a half.

Place a frying pan on a low heat and add the sugar. Once it starts to caramelize, add the water and simmer for around 8 minutes until treacle-like. Set aside.

Place a wok on a medium heat and add the coconut oil. Once sizzling, take the mixture and spoon into a piping bag. Gradually squeeze it out and, starting in the centre of the pan, carefully make a spiral in the hot oil. Fry until golden brown then remove and leave to sit in the caramel mix for around 5 minutes. Remove and leave to cool a little before serving.

SERVES: 4 PREP TIME: 90 COOKING TIME: 10

IMBUL KIRIBATH

4 tbsp brown sugar
¼ tsp salt
100g ground coconut
500g milk rice (see recipe on p360)

Place a frying pan on a low to medium heat and add the sugar and salt. Stir continuously until it turns into caramel. Add the ground coconut and stir thoroughly until combined. Remove from the heat and continue stirring for a couple of minutes.

Lay a piece of cling film on your work surface and place around half a cup of milk rice in the centre. Add 1-2 tablespoons of the caramelized coconut in a line, then roll like you would if making sushi, once rolled, twist both ends of cling film in different directions to tighten and bind the whole thing together.

Gently unwrap, making sure it doesn't fall apart and lose its shape, and cut in half to serve.

SERVES: 4 PREP TIME: 10 COOKING TIME: 10

SRI LANKAN COOKIES

50g caster sugar
75g melted butter
2 eggs
75g milk powder
1 tsp of vanilla bean paste
125g plain flour

FOR DUSTING:
25g melted butter
25g granulated sugar

Preheat your oven to 160C. Line a baking tray with baking paper.

Add the sugar, melted butter, eggs, milk powder and vanilla paste to a large mixing bowl. Mix together thoroughly and once combined add in the flour slowly, mixing until it is incorporated and you have a solid dough. If the mixture is too wet then add a little more flour.

Take a small amount of dough (a little bigger than the size of a golf ball) and roll in your hands into a ball shape. Then place onto your baking paper and flatten slightly with the palm of your hand. Repeat this process until all the dough is used up. Brush each dough ball with melted butter and sprinkle on the granulated sugar.

Bake for around 20-25 minutes or until golden brown on top. Remove from the oven, place on a cooling rack and serve once cooled.

SERVES: 4 PREP TIME: 10 COOKING TIME: 25

Buffalo curd for sale at the markets in
Galle on the South West coast.

Crafts & Culture

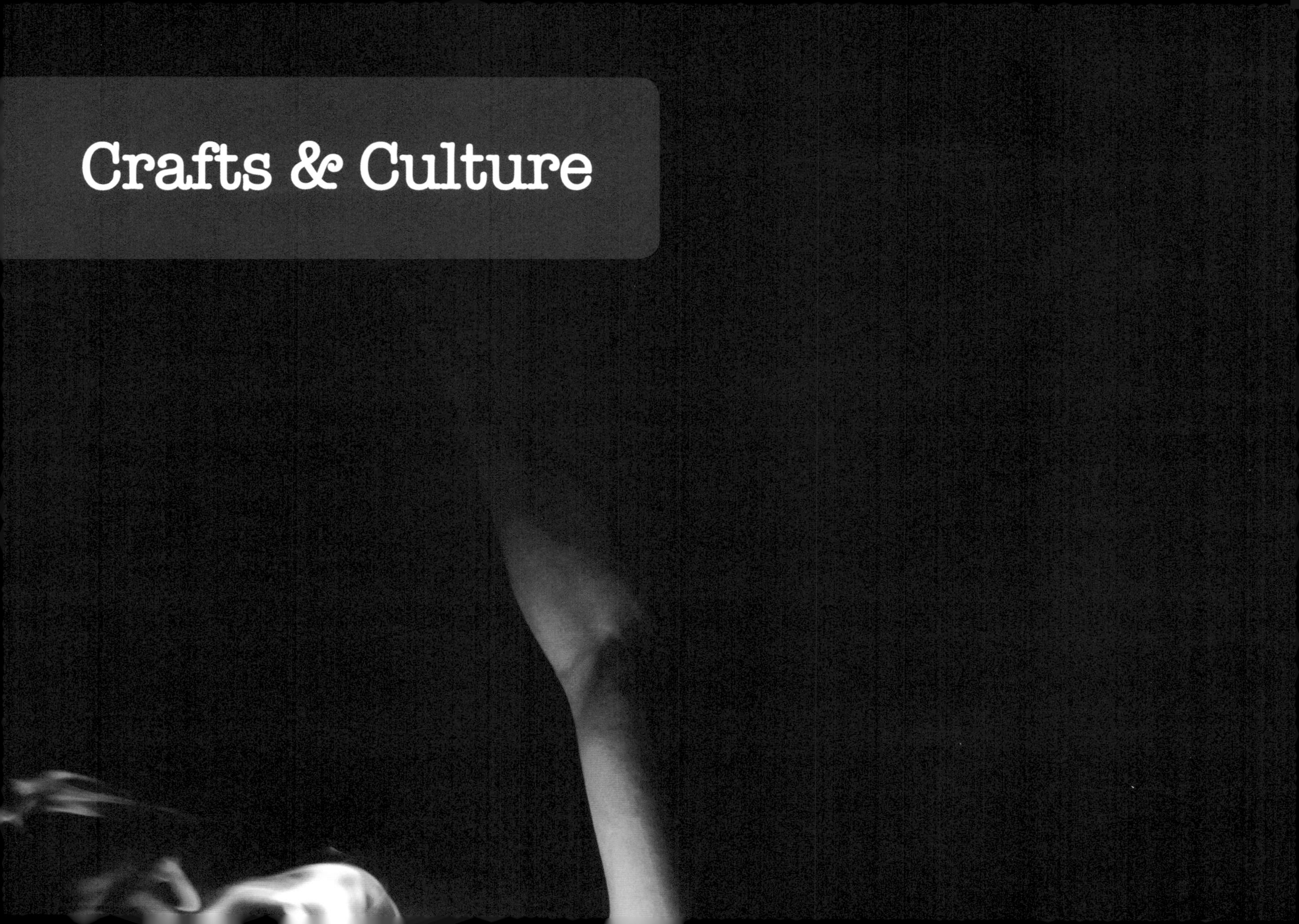

CRAFTS & CULTURE

Although predominantly Buddhist, Sri Lanka is a country with multicultural roots and welcomes all religions. In my experience, it is a land of religious freedom and tolerance, as shown through the national flag, in which the different colours and markings represent the main religious groups in the country.

Although I am not religious myself, the Buddhist philosophy and teachings are in line with my lifestyle and way of thinking. During my time in Sri Lanka, I have visited numerous Buddhist temples and have met many monks who have helped me along my journey to this point.

Sri Lankan masks are part of the island's rich and ancient heritage. Traditionally, they're made from kaduru wood as it is known for its softness and durability. Head to Ambalangoda on the south west coast to get a look at the talented craftsmen who produce each mask by hand. I'd also recommend that you check out the native batiks: they're amazing!

The Monks of Koggala Temple
on the way to prayers.

THECOOKS

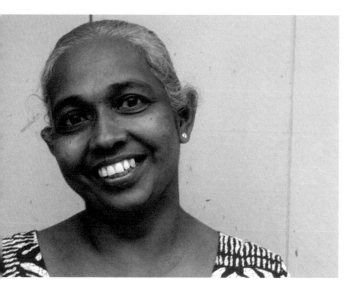 

RANJI

Ranji Panditha has been my Ski Lankan mum for the last decade and was one of the first faces I came across when I set foot on the island. A beautiful, happy, smiling woman with a heart of gold, Ranji was born in Baddegama, just inland on the south-west coast and grew up helping her mother cook delicious traditional recipes from a very young age.

At the age of 30, Ranji married Noel (my Sri Lankan dad), and in the late 70s they set up the Surfing Beach Guest House right on the beach overlooking Hikkaduwa's main surf break. Their popular guesthouse was one of the first around. In peak season, Ranji serves up her traditional recipes for up to 60 people a day at the guesthouse. Her food is delicious and I've been very fortunate to have enjoyed it for the last 10 years.

Try out the west coast recipes – they're all from Ranji.

ANOMA

One of the loveliest women I have ever met, Anoma is the eldest of three children, and from a young age watched her family cooking. These traditional skills and recipes were passed down through the generations.

At the age of 23, Anoma married Jayathunga and they bought a piece of land in Tissamaharma, in the south east of Sri Lanka. In 2004, they set up the successful Elephant Camp Guest House. From here, Jaya can organise a trip to Yala National Park with some of the best guides on the island.

Anoma is a talented and passionate cook, who has developed her traditional Sri Lankan cooking methods over the years. She grows all of her own vegetables, and aspires to teach cooking classes in the future. Taste the recipes and see for yourself – the east coast recipes are all straight from her kitchen.

NIKKI

Nikki was born in Nuwara Eliya in 1982, and moved to Wewala, Hikkaduwa to open a restaurant and hotel near the beach (Vibration on Galle Road – you can't miss it). She's super friendly and has two beautiful sons with her husband, Janika (Kulina, her eldest son, assisted on many of my photoshoots at their place).
Nikki is an excellent cook, and as with most Sri Lankan women, learnt the majority of her skills from her mother, father, and other members of the family.

JAYANTHA

Jayantha was born in the small village of Maraguamuwa in 1958. As with most Sri Lankan families, Jayantha's mother was the person who passed down traditional methods of cooking to him and he learnt many skills from watching her in the kitchen. Jayantha has been cooking at Ranjith's Beach Hut, overlooking Hikkaduwa's main surf break, for over 25 years. He is a super mellow guy with a very relaxed cooking style and no one makes a Sri Lankan prawn curry like he does. If he's not in the kitchen, you'll find him playing checkers with his buddy Kamal.

BIRANGA

This talented family man has been cooking since he was a teenager, learning his skills from his mother and father. He soon found work as a chef and has worked in kitchens ever since. He is a knowledgeable fisherman and sources his own ingredients regularly and his palette is second to none. Biranga is the master of seafood, and the delicious crab dish (see p138) is just one of his many recipes.

VINDI

A lovely guy and a firm friend, Vindika was born in Sri Lanka's cultural centre of Kandy in 1982. The youngest of two sons, he watched and helped his mother in the kitchen from early on and she taught him everything he knows when it comes to food and drink. As a cookery teacher, his mum cooks up all sorts of local recipes and delicious treats on a daily basis. Vindi took what he'd learnt about food and found a job near the beach, in Wewala. You can find Vindi shaking up delicious juices, lassis and cocktails for all to enjoy at Funky de Bar.

HEMWARTHI

Born in Walapene in Central Province, Sri Lanka, Hemawathi now lives in Nuwara Eilya, among the rolling highlands of the tea country. She started cooking at a young age with her mother, and quickly picked up the skills to cook all sorts of traditional recipes. You will often find Hemawathi's husband Samarakoon in the kitchen, helping out and joking around. They are a truly lovely family. At 55, Hemawathi is still passionate about her cooking, and has passed this knowledge and love of food down to her daughter.

GAYANI

Although Gayani was born and raised in the Matale district of Sri Lanka, she now lives in Birmingham in the UK with her son. Most of Gayani's childhood memories are related to food and she learnt her craft at a young age from her grandma and other relatives. Gayani is a bubbly character and a natural in the kitchen and she runs pop-up restaurants, hosts super clubs and makes and sells her own unique blend of curry powder.

THE LOCALS COOKBOOK TRAVEL KITCHEN

Recipe testing is key to any cookbook and The Locals' Cookbook is no exception.

Welcome to The Locals' Cookbook Travel Kitchen. This little van is where the recipes in this book were tested and spice blends conjured up. To date, I have trialled these recipes on over 500 people from all corners of the globe.

The Test Kitchen also doubled up as my home for a year whilst living in New Zealand back in 2013, with a domestic kitchen (albeit an extremely compact one that goes 50km to the gallon), a mobile herb garden, a fully stocked spice rack and every cooking utensil known to man. There was even a studio in which I wrote the recipes, edited the photos and finalised the design of the book.

Thank you to everyone who has been involved in helping to create The Locals' Cookbook.

The Locals Cookbook Travel Kitchen
ready for action back in 2013 in
Raglan, New Zealand.

THE FOOD TRUCK

Following the success of the travel kitchen I am hugely excited to be collaborating on The Locals' Cookbook with Bristol - based Sustainable Kitchens, a company with whom I share a passion for the colourful and independent people in this city and a core belief that by giving back to a community we can really make a difference.

Our plans together going forward are to take The Locals' Cookbook on the road with a fully equipped food truck/field kitchen and to host some fun cook-ups in the Sustainable Kitchens showroom – so look for our tasty UK tour coming soon.

"From the instant we first met Jon and saw an early draft of his beautiful book we were completely hooked. A travel cookbook with a beguiling story to tell, complete with incredible photography and unbelievable recipes, aimed entirely at giving back to the people who had inspired so much in him – we just wanted to help Jon in any way we could." Sam Shaw, Director at Sustainable Kitchens.

GLOSSARY
INGREDIENTS, EQUIPMENT AND SUPPLIERS

You will be able to find most of the ingredients for the recipes in this book in supermarkets (look out for the 'world food' section) or Asian supermarkets. The internet is useful for more difficult to source, specialty ingredients:

theasiancookshop.co.uk (Maldive fish flakes, goraka, fresh pandan leaves)
souschef.co.uk (urid/urad dal, fenugreek)
ukpola.com (goraka)

CURRY LEAVES

Curry leaves are grown all over Sri Lanka and add a very subtle yet distinctive flavour to a wide variety of dishes. Here in the UK, fresh curry leaves have been banned for the time being due to failure to comply with EU standards but they can be bought frozen or dried from most supermarkets.

FENUGREEK SEEDS

These cuboid, yellow to amber coloured seeds are frequently encountered in Sri Lankan cuisine and are used both whole and powdered. To extract the best flavour, the seeds are dry roasted.

GORAKA

This sour spice is commonly used as a thickening agent in South Indian and Sri Lankan cuisine. It is both acidic and fruity in flavour and is used mainly in meat and fish curries. If you can't find it, you could try substituting tamarind.

GREEN CAPSICUMS

Also known as banana peppers or banana chillis, these are a medium-sized member of the chilli pepper family that has a mild, tangy taste. While typically bright yellowish green, it is possible for them to change to green, red, or orange as they ripen. They can be substituted with green peppers if you are unable to find them.

GREEN CHILLIES

I use the Dutch variety, long slender chillies usually between 10-15 cm long with a distinct point at one end. They have a medium spiciness so won't blow your head off. Do wash your hands after handling chillies and whatever you do, don't put your hands anywhere near your eyes!

MALDIVE FISH FLAKES

A variety of cured tuna that is traditionally produced in the Maldives and made by boiling, smoking and then sun-drying the fish. You can substitute with shrimp paste or you can always just leave it out.

RAMPE /PANDANUS LEAF

These long slender leaves have a very aromatic flavour and are used in a wide variety of dishes. Pandan/rampe can be bought fresh, frozen or dried (but fresh is always best).

SHALLOTS

I use the smaller variety found in Asian supermarkets but you can substitute regular shallots (with 4 smaller shallots being roughly equivalent to 1 regular shallot).

URID/URAD DHAL

These lentil-like beans have black skins covering creamy white interiors. In Sri Lankan cuisine, the dhal is skinned and split and are creamy white in colour. They can be used whole or ground up into flour.

The following items will also be available from thelocalscookbook.com

COCONUT GRINDERS

This is an invaluble tool in any Sri Lankan kitchen and is used to grind out the flesh from inside a coconut. Available from **spicesofindia.co.uk**

KOKIS MOULDS

These are used to make a very popular Sri Lankan dessert. Available from **kapruka.com**

NON-STICK HOPPER PANS

These pans are used to make hoppers, a sort of rice flour crepe, sometimes made with an egg in the centre and usually eaten for breakfast. Available from **amazon.co.uk**

STRING HOPPERS PRESS

These presses are used to make string hoppers, a staple in the Sri Lankan diet. They are quite hard to come by in the UK but you can substitute it with a Sev Sancha Pasta maker. Available from **amazon.co.uk**

One of my favourite views in the world,
Surfing Beach Guesthouse at Sunset.

ACKNOWLEDGEMENTS

Right then, it has been a long time from concept to publication, so this is a lengthy list. Apologies if I've missed anyone out, but thank you to:

Ranji, Anoma, Nikki, Jayantha, Biranga, Gayani, Vindi, and Hemwarthi for providing me with their delicious and authentic recipes.

Sam, Charlie and Nicky at Sustainable Kitchens for their ongoing support and for believing in this project. Without them, none of this would be possible.

My beautiful girlfriend Dominique for supporting me all the way and for putting up with my five year obsession with getting this series off the ground.

For their constant support and advice, I'd like to thank Borra Garson, Rob Allison, Jaynie Bye, Sophie Alcock and Mandy Davey.

Sophie Missing for all her hard work and for turning my ramblings into something special.

For always believing in me and supporting me, I'd like to thank my Dad, Trish and my brother Nick, Natalie and the rest of the Bowdens, the Thomson Family, Noel and Hasanka Panditha, Pinnith, Johan and Linn, Saya, Nisanka and the boys at Funky de Bar, Bunta, Baddegama Samitha, Baddegama Ariyadhamma, Jaya, Paul, Helen, Zoe and Jamie at Devol.

For supplying me with the finest ingredients: M.J Dalton Butchers, Three Wise Monkeys Grocers, The Fish Shop, Tovey's Seafood (all in Bristol), Tucker's Fresh Fish, Coakley-Green Fishmongers and Exotic Foods (all in Swansea).

I'd also like to say a huge thank you to Emily Mounter and Chris Cooper for allowing me to take over their kitchen to test, cook and shoot all of the recipes in this book.

Kaspar at Phasefour Media and Carl at Holy Moly Creative for helping to tidy up my design work.

And last but not least, all my Bristol crew, my Swansea crew and all my other friends from around the world for their ongoing support.

It's been a crazy journey but I wouldn't have it any other way. Much love and respect to everyone involved!